# Keeping the Kids All Right

*How to Empower Your Children
Against the Leftist Agenda—
Without Homeschooling*

# BARAK LURIE

CT3Media, Inc., Los Angeles, CA

ISBN: 979-8-85179-166-6

*For permission requests, write to:*
CT3Media, Inc.
12100 Wilshire Boulevard, 8th Floor
Los Angeles, CA 90025
www.ct3media.com/

Jacket design: Envelop Video

Interior typesetting and eBook: Lisa Parnell

Printed in the United States of America

*For Alex Lurie*

# TABLE OF CONTENTS

*"It is easier to build strong children than to repair broken adults."*

— Frederick Douglas

*Train up a child in the way he should go; even when he is old, he will not depart from it.*

— Proverbs 22:6 esv

# INTRODUCTION

I t's enough to terrify you.

You love God. You love America and see her as the beacon of liberty, freedom, and justice. You know the impact America has had in world history. You still get the chills of pride when you hear the Star-Spangled Banner play. You may even go to pro-life, pro-America, and pro-God rallies.

You grimace as you see the cultural wars play out—the demonizing of America, the relaxing of drug and crime enforcement and the glorification of drugs, the explosion and apparent encouragement of sexuality in the schools, the dismissal of marriage and family as central institutions, and the toxification of masculinity. Merely mentioning God sends school administrators into a tizzy as though you're denying global warming, questioning the need for the Covid vaccine, and yelling the n-word on a bullhorn all at the same time.

But the good news—at least you think—is that our kids embrace what we embrace. They love waving that American flag at that conservative caravan and rally, too. They love God and Jesus, too. All is good with the world.

That is, until they reach puberty. Often, it's earlier.

The schools get to them. Social media and liberal news outlets get to them. Their friends, porn, and strange new ideas that peddle easy answers get to them. These factors all use powerful and appealing messaging of tolerance and compassion

1

to others. They tell your child to think inclusively, and that there are no real distinctions among any people at all. They even encourage kids not to tell parents what they might have encouraged the children to think: That they might be non-binary or gay, or that they should at least explore their sexuality and sex itself. *You need to learn about birth control, Bella. Your mom and dad may never support you on this, but we do. We're not backward, like they are.*

Suddenly, you realize you're in a war with the teachers in your kids' school, and the battleground is your kids' minds. The race is on to see who will get there first.

But soon it feels like a fools' endeavor, like you're running to catch up with the sun.

It's worse than you think: There's a new mindset. Educators see themselves as "experts." You must genuflect to whatever they teach your kids. Better yet, think of them as gods.

They know better, think better, and understand better. They—not you—are the only ones entitled to shape your kids. Parents have no business in shaping what teachers teach their children, and if they don't like that, they can go elsewhere.

This is exactly what happened in a New Jersey school board meeting in late 2022, when parents met to express their outrage over the district's transgender policy. The school board's lawyer told them that it was "not the right of the parents to determine the curriculum taught to their children at public schools," and that they should go elsewhere if they didn't like it. Never mind that they're teaching the same garbage everywhere else.

Parents attending the Lawrence Township Board of Education meeting had come to the school board meeting to express concern over lessons and books with gender-questioning themes. One of the books in controversy was *Jacob's New Dress* by Ian and Sarah Hoffman. It was a picture book for kindergartners, and it tells the story of a young boy who enjoys playing dress-up and wants to wear a dress to school. *And what's wrong with that? Absolutely nothing.*

Parents also confronted the district about encouraging fourth-grade students to question their gender with a lesson on the "gender snowperson." Students were also asked to play a game where they could explore any gender they chose.

Parents also challenged the district's transgender policy, Policy 5756, which states that the district "shall accept a student's asserted gender identity" and that they are not required to "notify a student's parent of the student's gender identity or expression." The district was also to include instruction "on the political, economic, and social contributions of persons with disabilities and lesbian, gay, bisexual, and transgender people, in an appropriate place in the curriculum of middle school and high school students."[1]

If only it would stop there. Behind your back, educators may characterize your belief system as evil. At best they'll tell your kids you're just backward folks that haven't quite yet stepped into the 21st century. They'll say you're still stuck in the mud of 20th century thinking. Such a funny image, imagining one's parents stuck in the mud, trying pathetically to get one leg out at a time. In their heads, the children see themselves speeding past their parents on a highway in their eco-friendly electric Ferrari. What a contrast! Plus, there's the added advantage of making the kids feel superior and more intelligent than their parents.

They'll do it in every arena that's important to you: They'll advance anti-Americanism, anti-Christianity, anti-Western civilization, anti-masculinity, anti-capitalism, and anti-population growth.

While they're bringing those down, they'll prop up transgenderism and the related teaching of sexuality at earlier and earlier ages, global warming, evolution, socialism, and the redefining of history, particularly the Constitution and the "real" intent behind it. Everything should be seen in the context of race (Critical Race Theory), or some "intersectionality" (whatever *that* means). Oh, and be very, very careful with your pronouns. You've been making a lot of assumptions and *all* of them are offensive.

Abortions are not only acceptable, but a reclamation of noble independence and fierce individuality. Religion is at odds with Science—and you're not against *Science*, are you? So make your Sophie's Choice now.

Marriage was for older generations that didn't know better, and we're all past that patriarchal form of suffocation, thank you. And finally, the government should do everything for us. Big business is bad, and all regulations are good. Unions, minimum wage, and government loan forgiveness are essential if we truly want society to grow. Drugs are good, law enforcement is bad. In fact, defund the police.

There is no "good" nor "evil." In fact, one shouldn't describe anything in terms of good or bad—'cause it might hurt someone's feelings. Well, except if you're talking about those nice transgendered folk. They're all good, even when they're engaging in those mass shooting sprees.

Our elite twenty-something year-old know-betters also demand that we reexamine all former taboos: polyamorous relationships; same-sex marriage; polygamy; and of course pedophilia I mean minor-attracted persons. And you know what? Incest might be okay, too. (Just wait, you'll see.)

And no one—under any circumstances whatsoever— should *ever* be made to feel "less than" or bad about themselves in any manner. Unless you're a Trump-supporter, conservative, Christian, or white. Or a straight I mean cis-gender boy. Then you can wail on those like William Wallace avenging the killing of his wife in that first attack scene in *Braveheart*. If you're any combination of those things then your concerns are about as important to your school administrators as the protection of minor girls was at Epstein Island.

It's worse than that. If your child is guilty of being any of those things, he becomes a punching bag for all the other kids. *There's one of those bigoted, homophobic, binary, slavery-loving and anti-science Christians right there!*

You say Little Johnny doesn't want to be a punching bag? No problem. All he needs to do is shut up. And if he does that, Johnny will be able to withstand all that social pressure. Everyone knows kids are *awesome* at resisting social pressure.

You might as well have let thugs break into your house and kidnap your kids from their bedrooms, never to see them again. But it's worse: You're bringing them *to* the kidnappers, day after day, for at least six hours a day.

It doesn't have to be this way. Intuitively, you know it yourself. But what can you do? You figure you could just keep them cloistered at home, and home-school them for years and years. You could shut them off from all social media, friends and everyone else. But that would be like shutting down the world's economy just to stop the spread of some new virus. But that would be an absurd example, I suppose.

Make no mistake: The new woke culture *is* a virus, and just like a virus, its agenda is to spread itself far and wide. Suddenly, you feel like one of the survivalists seeking refuge in an isolated "safe-zone" town during a zombie apocalypse. Will the virus spread to your children?

Again: It doesn't have to be this way. This book will show you how.

Let's stay with the virus analogy for now. There are many highly contagious viruses. And yet, you and I know many people who seem almost never to get sick. You, however, seem to get a cold every couple of months (or the dreaded Covid-19 virus that the vaccine—*thank God for Science*—has managed to immunize everyone from ever contracting it again except when they do contract it).

What are these lucky people doing (or not doing) that helps them ward off such diseases? Do they eat better? Do they exercise a lot? Do they meditate or take some sort of strict regimen of anchovies and garlic?

It almost doesn't matter. What *does* matter is that such people exist. All it takes is asking those people what they're doing or not doing which they say helps them ward off viruses. Maybe if you mimic them, you too can enjoy a life where sickness is alien to your body too.

And the same thing applies to many parents of kids—kids the same age as your own. You know whom I'm talking about: They're the parents who seem to have it all, at least in the raising of their kids. These parents seem never to worry, even though they're sending their kids to the very same school.

And you just *know* that these kids are going to be fine. They're already well-behaved, self-motivated, and apprecia-tive of their country, their faith, and their parents. The parents don't even seem to think very much about it. They act like a crew flying through a hurricane in one of those C-130 Hercules "Hurricane Hunter" planes: They literally fly right into the hur-ricanes, but the crazy winds don't really phase them. They just power through it, while feeling barely a jostle.

Maybe those parents *seem* to handle the situations perfectly, and you know intuitively in your head that no one can have everything under control. But still, they've got game, and you want in. They must know something you don't know.

So what explains their success? What are they doing that you're not doing? Why are you fretting day after day, while they seem to go about their lives, confident in every way in their kids' success in school, athletics, social life—and future?

It's all about developing and sticking to a process. As we progress in this book, we'll discuss what *won't* work as much as what *will* work. Then I will propose the steps you should take. They are ultimately the *only* steps by which this can work. If you follow them, you will forever safeguard your kids—immu-nize them, as it were—from the woke culture for as long as they live.

If you follow these steps, your kids will be just as animated as you to protect the legacy of God, America, and Western Civ-ilization in their own lives and in their broader community.

And when they have their own kids (and they'll actually want to have kids), they'll share your passion to safeguard their kids the same way.

And a warning: don't do this half-way. Just like you wouldn't follow just half a recipe when you're baking something, you'll need to follow *all* the steps. The good news is that the steps are simple and doable.

The bottom line is not to repeat the mistakes of so many others who take the fear-based approach of anger, fretting, and ineffective activism.

You'll only end up banging your head against the wall. That's neither good for your head nor the wall.

# CHAPTER I

# THE PROBLEM

"A government is like everything else: to preserve it, we must love it," wrote the French philosopher Montesquieu. "Everything, therefore, depends on establishing this love in a republic. [Inspiring] it ought to be the principal business of education."

As a younger man, Thomas Jefferson quoted these words into his "commonplace book," a private journal he kept as a student for future inspiration. He believed teaching children American history should be *the* primary goal of public schools.

A few years after Jefferson wrote the Declaration of Independence and helped win the nation's freedom, he made a commitment to the words he had once inscribed in his notebook. He launched a campaign to establish a free public education system, a central tenet in his plan for the continued vibrancy of America's young democracy. For children aged 6 to 8, he wrote, the study of American history should be a central focus of the school day. This would ensure that these future citizens would cherish the republic the Founders had won for them. He believed by learning this history, they would make proper decisions for America's future.

All that has changed. As education expert Michael J. Petrilli argues, schools now instead chase higher graduation rates, college-enrollment numbers and top standardized-test scores—and the demonizing of America and advocating for its dismantling.

Common Core standards, which the Obama administration pushed throughout the country, ignited a furious backlash from many parents and teachers, who found that technocratic education reforms led to a "vacuous mania for the mechanics of math and reading." It also taught "reading comprehension with no content, … which rendered it as boring and ineffective as it sounds."[2]

There's far less emphasis on the Founding Fathers, Shakespeare, Mark Twain, John Hume, or classical music composers. There is *no* discussion of the contributions of Judaism, Christianity, America, or Western Civilization—except for their contributions of slavery, racism, patriarchy, homophobia, and something new called "transphobia," which is just as big and bad as slavery ever was.

At best, such things have become afterthoughts, something to be taught only if and when they get through all the other more important topics. Alas, with all that godlessness, evolution, abortion rights, gay and other minority rights, and global warming advocacy to pursue, there's just so little time in the day left.

Many adults today under forty don't even know when America declared independence from Britain. Go ahead. Ask any American born after 1980. Nine out of ten times, he or she won't have the slightest clue. He won't even know it was Britain from which we declared that independence. Generally speaking, the tenth one will be a conservative.

Jefferson might say this of our public schools of today: You had one job — and you failed.[3]

Then again, students in Jefferson's day didn't have to learn the 1619 Project. That controversial effort, which the know-betters at the *New York Times* launched in 2019, is a wholesale reinterpretation of America's founding, seeking to undo every ideal that you might have otherwise held about it. To hear it from the *Times*, our national history is racist to the core, rooted in slavery and white supremacy. To advance this inversion of American history, they published a 100-page magazine "supplement" to the nation's standard history curriculum. More than 3,500 American high schools adopted it.[4]

As Petrilli put it: "[The 1619 Project] is a perfect example of what has gone so wrong in American schools when it comes to history. It isn't teaching history, warts and all; it's just the warts." It's the latest in a long line of critical revisions of the American story, going back to Howard Zinn's influential *A People's History of the United States*. That book, published in 1980, aimed to tell "US history from the ground up" (whatever that means), and stripped American history of its traditional heroes, and for that matter anything positive America had done. In many states, a single high-school history class is the only civics instruction that future voters ever receive. Eight states don't even make the study of American history a graduation requirement. Worse yet, as Petrilli describes it, "We're telling our young people that America is racist and oppressive and has only failed over the years to do right by the most vulnerable, rather than that we were founded with incredible ideals that we have sometimes failed to live up to."[5]

As Stanford University professor Chester E. Finn, Jr. writes in his book *How to Educate an American: The Conservative Vision for Tomorrow's Schools* (2020), we no longer teach "patriotic" history, or hold on to any sense that active citizenship must derive from a sense of civic purpose, a positive attachment to one's society. It was a feeling the ancient Greeks called patriotism. It is this sense of attachment and identification that makes democratic participation meaningful. As he wrote, "to acquire civic purpose, students need to care about their country."[6]

All that now is slipping away. Many attribute the rapid demise to the return of soldiers from World War II, who had seen the world's greatest devastation imaginable, and in the aftermath just wanted to settle into a peaceful future without talk of the war horrors they had just seen. Teaching their kids about the values of America was less important. Ironically, such teaching would have helped avoid another such horrific world war.

Still others attribute a much longer historically systematic scheme in the stripping of America's Christian and biblical roots from the public education system. It started in the late 1800s with atheist John Dewey and later the NEA union. Then there was the 1962 Supreme Court decision in *Engel vs Vitale*, striking down government sponsored prayers, which led to more aggressive prohibitions of *any* form of prayer in schools in the decades that followed.

It got to the point that even bringing up God in schools became as toxic as misgendering Bruce I mean Caitlyn Jenner. Administrators and other faculty simply took the High Court's interpretation all the way and assumed that *any* mention of God at all—even in historical context—was a violation of the First Amendment. So better safe than sorry and pretend God had never been a factor in history, culture, or society at all. Except for all the bad stuff.

Perhaps all these elements contributed and fed off one another. Whatever the cause, the result has been the same: the creation of an environment that scrubs out conservative, American and God-based teaching, while amplifying atheism, evolution, and other secular agendas—none of which fell into the category of "offensive" religion.

Think of it: there's nothing unconstitutional about teaching transgenderism or even encouraging a child to think of himself as a girl. There's nothing unconstitutional about teaching that bad guys founded America to perpetuate slavery, that evolution explains our origins, that the universe created itself, and that Christianity has killed and destroyed more than anything else in the history of earth. In fact, there's plenty of banter that the Founding Fathers set up America not only as a secular country, but an atheist country. Indeed, perhaps the Founding Fathers were atheists themselves! Either way it's cool because lefties gets to wrap themselves up with the Constitution when it destroys Christianity and God, while simultaneously dismissing it as toilet paper because the Founding Dads created it solely to perpetuate slavery and racism.

Regardless, the absolute red-line that the cultural leftists have created is that you can't teach a child that God has been central to our morality and civilization, or monotheism was the primary basis for our civilization. *That* particular dog won't hunt.

So you feel like Snoopy being excluded from this or that store or restaurant while that song *No Dogs Allowed* plays in the background. The new no-God dogma creates an insurmountable obstacle in the schools: a bouncer at the nightclub who only lets in whom he wants to let in. By creating a paranoia that any mention of God might lead to a lawsuit, the Left effectively could oust any whiff of God from class.

No school district wants to lawyer up and pay hundreds of thousands of dollars to lawyers to defend Judaism or Christianity. Many of the district administrators are not so keen on God anyway. The school just wants to pump out kids at graduation.

Even those administrators who might prefer some invocation of God in the classroom figure the kids can get all that religious stuff at home or Church on Sunday, right? They themselves see education and religion as separate. So who's really out there, championing the cause of religion, freedom, and America? Cue the wispy desert breeze and rolling tumbleweeds now.

Schools might as well put up a big neon sign in front and make it obvious: *No God allowed.*

But there *is* cause for hope: parents are pushing back, successfully. It's a slog, but more conservatives are getting elected or at least participating in school boards. We may be behind, and it will likely take a lot more work.

Publishers have also put out more books for children on history themes, everything from straightforward biographies of important Americans to graphic novels like "Nathan Hale's Hazardous Tales," which retell stories like the battle of the

Alamo, World War I and II, and more. There's also the Tuttle Twins and Brave Books, among many others. PragerU Kids creates videos geared to children on a multitude of conservative and pro-American topics.

Then there was *Hamilton,* an enormously entertaining Broadway musical which gave us a patriotic and inspiring telling of the early days of the Republic. Most significant, it was *accurate.* Slavery figured in the story, too, but in context. Lin Manuel showed how society even back then hotly debated it. The Revolution was not, as the 1619 Project would have us believe, a war to perpetuate or "save" slavery. The play's focus was the Founders' ideal of freedom, and how this ideal was revolutionary even back then. There was no mistaking that this ideal would one day extend greater freedoms for all.

Despite this riveting musical retelling of the most critical years of America's birth and the mass appeal of its message, few teachers use it as a guide for their students. Despite the fact that children naturally gravitate toward belonging and a sense of connection to a past with noble ideals, *Hamilton*'s narrative doesn't jibe with the very different historical narrative they want to advance.

The truth is, teachers would rather have children dulled and disaffected, purposeless and aimless, than to have them enthusiastic and patriotic. "Educators have all but abandoned the mission of creating an *e pluribus unum*, of instilling a sense of common history and culture," Manhattan Institute's Kay Hymowitz points out in another essay in the Petrilli book. Instead, there is a devotion to diversity that only pulls us farther apart than ever before.[7]

Citizenship and a love of our history is the number one reason why we developed a public school system in the first place. We have lost that. Ironically, far from teaching *e pluribus Unum*, it is this same public school system that the progressive left has now hijacked to disavow any greatness in America, to encourage hatred of it, and to separate us into balkanized *Lord of the Flies*-type factions.

Ironically, part of what has awakened parents came from an unlikely source: the shutdown of in-school learning resulting from the Covid-19 pandemic of 2020-21. For the first time, many parents saw what their kids were learning. Teachers even wanted to prevent parents from frustrating their mission in brainwashing the kids.[8]

It was eye-opening for many parents. It was one thing to hear about schools pushing woke agendas on their kids in the abstract, it was quite another to actually see it happen in living color. It was the difference between hearing about crime statistics in your city on the TV, and actually getting mugged.

That's the way a lot of parents understood the woke issues: they knew it was happening in this or that school, but probably not *their* kids' school. And if it *was* happening in their school, it was only one agenda-driven rogue teacher that didn't speak for the rest of the school. *Not Johnny's teacher. My Johnny would tell me about it, and I would make a stink.*

But there they were—teachers actually preaching their progressive religion upon your kids. Suddenly, parents were "shocked, shocked" to hear what their kids' teachers were saying, right there in their living room. Wokism became real to them. They could see it flipping the lid on their kids' brains and reaching in with their mind-numbing tentacles.

It felt like one of those horror movies where the mad scientist attaches electrodes onto the sides of his trapped victim's head. He switches the voltage on, and pretty soon the patient's brains will turn into some zombie mush, or he'll be converted into yet another foot soldier for his ever-increasing empire. Soon the patient-victim will mouth off the empire's authoritarian slogans and will in turn convert others to the cause.

You panic. All of a sudden, you realize it may already be too late. And you don't even know where or how to start. Suddenly, you realize you're way behind. You didn't even know you were in a race. You missed the starting gun.

You don't have to be that parent. With this book, you won't be.

CHAPTER II

# WHAT WON'T WORK

Before getting into what works, it pays to look at what doesn't work. Then we'll discuss what does.

## Shelter from the Storm?

One option is to shelter your kids from all possible disagreeable influences. It's a strong and understandable instinct. You are above all a caring parent.

You are a knight at the gates of the fortress. You will be ever vigilant, ready for those barbarians. You'll build a Great Wall around your kids, like those ancient Chinese guys did for their country. Surely that will protect your kids from all those dangerous outside influences.

This won't work for several reasons. First, it's virtually impossible to keep out every influence. You might think you're like those Jedi knights fending off all those stormtrooper laser bullets, but you can only swing your arms so fast.

Even if you turn off every TV in the house and prohibit every smart device and access to every computer, do you really think they won't see Snapchat, TikTok and Instagram posts from their friends at school or elsewhere? The only way to truly do that is to prevent them from having any regular friends at all—no playdates, no club sports, no unsupervised visits to the mall—or only associate with like-minded families. It might work if you're Amish, but otherwise it will ultimately only create festering resentment in your kids, as they begrudge you for isolating them from everyone else.

For another, there is only so much time in the day: You *do* have to work. You simply cannot be there for them every hour of the day, let alone monitor all their activities. You'll exhaust yourself and may even ultimately resent your kids. The kids will sense that. They'll also lose any sense of independence and experiencing of the world on their own; a value you as a conservative should want to foster, not squelch.

Worse, you'll project an atmosphere of fear. It won't take long before your kids will internalize this fear themselves, sticking on them like marijuana smoke at a Lollapaloosa concert. Fear is also exactly the *opposite* of what you want to convey in this whole process: Fear discourages risk-taking, innovation and creativity, and otherwise erodes one's energy to resist evil.

And it might actually pay to learn from the Great Wall of China. It ultimately failed, at least in its intended goal: When you build a wall over 4,000 miles long, you expect to keep at least some pesky nomadic raiders out. But marauding armies repeatedly managed to breach the Wall.

Interestingly, the Mongol Yuan Dynasty (1271–1368) overran the Wall and took over the whole of China from the Song Dynasty. Then those same Mongols used the Wall themselves as their *own* defensive line. One imagines the vanquished leaders of the Song Dynasty, spending their final horrific moments before being slaughtered, rubbing their chins and appreciating the irony of it all.[9]

## Taking It to the Man

Well then, you tell yourself, I'll just go straight to the principal, and demand—*demand*—that the school not teach any of that CRT or transgender crap. In your mind's eye, you see yourself knocking some proverbial heads. What a great dad or mom you'll be! You'll threaten them with all sorts of things, although you're not sure with what yet. You'll figure that out later. You'll talk about what you want out of the education of your child—it should be only about reading, writing, and 'rithmetic; and what so wrong about teaching them a little about God? It's the way *you* were taught. Kids need these basic foundations to succeed in an ever-competitive environment, you argue.

In your mind's eye, you sure look like one tough hombre. The principal will have no choice but to back down once he sees the sincerity of your convictions.

Here's how you see it playing out:

*You: Listen, Principal McGinnis, I love the school, but my little Teddy is telling me that the school is teaching critical race theory, and that boys and girls are one and the same. He even says his math teacher claims math is rooted in white privilege, invented by old white men from Europe. This just ain't right, dammit. (You pound your fist on his table). Things have GOT to change.*

*Principal (positively shocked): My goodness, tell me more. (Principal pulls out a pad and pencil to make sure he gets this right).*

*You (getting more animated): Well yes, there IS more. Teddy's history teacher says that God is a fabrication, an opiate of the masses. He also thinks that America is the worst country on earth, invented slavery, and that capitalism needs to be demolished.*

*Principal (shaking his head and heaving a sigh of deep concern): I had no idea. I can't tell you how much I appreciate your coming in and bringing this to my attention.*

*You: (getting up and shaking his hand): Well, I'm so pleased we had this meeting. Thank you.*

*Principal: Oh, not more pleased than me that you took the time to come here and alert me to all this, Mr. Jenkins. And don't worry: the next time we meet, I think you'll find things will be VERY different, my friend. (Giving knowing look, clasping your right hand with both of his hands). VERY different, indeed.*

So you try to have that meeting. You know you just can't barge into his office, so you call and ask for a meeting with the principal. After much back-and-forth with his secretary, it actually takes weeks to get a meeting with him. He can only meet you between 8:45 AM and 9 AM on Tuesdays or Thursdays. So whatever you want to say, you better make it fast.

Then you meet. You've planned it out all the prior week with your wife and perhaps even with your kids (who are just *mortified* that you're going to do this and embarrass them). No matter: The big moment is upon you.

Well, it's not at all like you've imagined. He hears you, yes, but he's looking at his watch all the time. He's distracted about some other item on his agenda: a meeting with the teacher's union later that afternoon, some skirmish that happened at the gym with some students that *sounded* racist, or perhaps a call he needs to make to lock in a generous donation from a woke parent of another student. All the while, his secretary keeps interrupting the meeting to tell him he's got calls. Some of them he pushes off, some of them he takes. *I'm so sorry. Excuse me just a minute. This won't take long.*

And even if you do ever get his attention, and even if he hears what you have to say, he'll roll his eyes—just a little bit—making clear that he's heard this complaint before. You're not presenting anything new to him. You sense he's about to push you off like he's pushed off everyone else: "Well," he finally says, standing up. "We have to consider the interests of everyone here, I hope you understand." He explains there are many parents who want a much more progressive agenda, and he has to accommodate them, too. But thank you for taking the time to meet with him! He thinks it's great you take an interest with the school curriculum. Stop by again anytime!

But he *does* do the double handclasp of your right hand.

Such efforts won't work. At best, the principal will request the teachers to be more balanced—whatever that means. So you'll have a teacher make a passing reference to "some people believe that God might have created the universe," or "some people believe that climate change is natural and human involvement doesn't really affect it." Then she'll cough loudly while simultaneously yelling "idiots!" It gets the young 'uns roaring with laughter. But they sure brought up the "other side of the argument," didn't they?

So it doesn't work if the teachers aren't themselves passionate about the same things you are. They'll resent you for forcing them to say anything, and they may very well take it out on your kid, like the waiter spitting in your soup when you send it back because it wasn't hot enough.

And these educators generally are much more passionate about *opposing* your patriarchal and misogynist views. (And racist. Never forget the racism). They're true believers. In their view, it's as if the school administration told them a couple of noisy German parents told them they needed to show Hitler's side of the "debate" on the Holocaust.

I challenge you to present a single time where a fed-up dad or mom succeeded in altering the school curriculum in any substantive way. Show me where a school has ever altered course and now is teaching the greatness of America. Show me a school where CRT and announcing your sexuality and gender identification and learning about sex toys and the latest gay sexual positions are nightmares of the past. Show me where global warming and evolution are out, and God, American history and limited government are in. Show me the great victory. Just one.

And whatever minor success you have, such as getting rid of an offensive, inappropriate library book, it will be short-lived. They'll take it out of the library and another woke teacher will re-introduce it or something very similar the next year. And don't forget the factor of time: these "successes" (such as they are) take months or even years before the school implements any corrective action—meaningless as it may be.

The bottom line: the change you'd like to happen is not going to happen. You might as well expect your dog to start giving you stock tips.

## City Hall and Other Things You Still Can't Fight

So taking it to the principal doesn't work. But you've got another arrow in your quiver. You'll go over the principal's head to some sort of School Board meeting, you will. That's where they'll *really* hear what you have to say.

Off you go. Now you're there, sitting in the chairs among ten or so other like-minded concerned parents. One by one you hear their stories. Some of them even come with a prepared speech from a crumpled paper in their back pocket. As you wait your turn, another parent plays back a recording of a woke teacher saying outrageous things about how students who don't think climate change is real are going to get penalized in their grades. Another parent holds up a book showing licentious photos in the third-grade section of the library. A student at a school board meeting reads aloud from another book in the library encouraging oral and anal sex.[10]

Finally, it's your turn. You nervously get up to that microphone and talk about how you don't like how they're dissing capitalism. You feel a bit embarrassed because the other parents' topics and stories are far more outrageous, but still, you're part of the angry mob now. Surely, this is where democracy thrives—at school board meetings.

The School Board members look back at you with just the same bored look you got from the principal. They, too, have heard all this before. But they sure appreciate your involvement and concern you've shown in the two minutes they've allotted you to speak. They assure you that they will certainly, almost definitely, quite possibly consider it when they develop a curriculum for the next academic year. They might even send you an email with more information about what they decide to do.

As you leave, you feel like a guest leaving Montgomery Burns' mansion in *the Simpsons*: *Ta-ta, Thanks for coming. Smithers, release the hounds.*

# Sue the Bastards

So you figure you'll sue the school. This is an avenue many parents have recently thought of pursuing on many fronts, particularly when it came to vaccine mandates which many schools imposed in 2021. On this issue, I received many calls from parents at my own children's schools: They knew I was a conservative ally, a recognized radio-show host of some stature, and a lawyer to boot. Maybe a lawsuit will finally get the schools to see they were serious. "This could be huge and have ripple effects all through the country," they insisted. *This could be the turning point!*

Well, not so much. There are two major problems I relay to any parents on this score: First, the chances of you drawing a judge who might share your views is at best, say, fifty-fifty. It's probably much worse than that in liberal areas like San Francisco, Los Angeles, and New York City. If you draw a left-leaning judge (and you likely will), she'll side with the progressive position. And,… scene.

Second, you can assert all the great legal arguments you want, but judges have a lot of discretion in interpreting facts, law, and in rendering judgments. As regards the vaccine mandate, for example, a judge might consider all the evidence showing that children are very unlikely to spread or get Covid-19, let alone in a manner which threatens their lives or others. You can "prove" that the mortality rate is minuscule and the cost/benefit and risks of the side effects of the vaccine compel the conclusion that the mandate is not only unconstitutional, but dangerous to children's health.

But it's easy for him to say that we're in a public health emergency, and that we all must do our part. And he can rely on whatever contrary evidence and experts the school offers.

Your case is over. And now you've not only burned a lot of bridges, but a lot of dough. And good luck getting little Johnny any references from the school's teachers later on when it's time for him to apply to middle or high school.

## The Great Accreditation Monster

Third, all your efforts may be for naught anyway. The teachers and the administrators all get marching orders from the state as to what they *must* teach. So even if the school might otherwise share all your positions on America, evolution, God, global warming and all the other social issues of the day, they won't get accreditation from the state if they defy what the state wants them to teach. As of 2021, for example, six states have laws requiring K-12 instructional materials to include and represent LGBTQ+ people and identities. (Fun fact: In Nevada, the mandate for inclusive content starts in kindergarten).[11]

Yes, a school can technically function without receiving accreditation, but even if every parent in the school fully agrees with a school's conservative-based agenda, they won't send their kids there if Johnny Law doesn't give the nod. In this sense, we are part of our own obstacles: we so desperately want to maximize our children's chances to go to the most recognized colleges, that we avoid grade schools that would teach our children exactly what we would want them to teach.

Like the cult followers of Jim Jones in Guyana, we wanted social acceptance so badly, we've indirectly imbibed the Kool-Aid, too. Even if we know it means the spiritual poisoning of our children.

## Haunted Houses Don't Want You in Them

Here's a question I ask many of my fretful parent friends: Why would you want to belong to a school which you don't like, and which doesn't like you? Isn't it like dating someone who's staying with you only because he feels like he has to?

People seem to have greater ease divorcing their spouses than divorcing their schools. With schools, their worry about the "trauma" that little Suzie or Tommy will suffer if they have to switch schools (*She'll miss all her friends! He's doing so well on his school tennis team. Switching him now, well… I just can't bear the thought of it.)*

Here's what I tell those parents. If you really can't stand it, then just *go*. Yes, just *go*. Most of these restless worries about what might happen if they move are not warranted. In my own life, my family moved a lot—often to different countries with different languages and cultures. My siblings and I ended up going to up to eight schools in seventeen years. Yet I looked forward to each move: Each one promised new adventures, new friends, new food, new *everything*. I not only survived but thrived. I learned a couple of languages along the way.

So leave. Depart. Exit. Skedaddle.

Just get out of there. Move to a different district, town, city or even state if you can't stand it there anymore. Think of it like you're in a haunted house movie, and the blood is dripping from the walls and a deep, loud echoey voice is repeatedly and ominously bellowing: "GET OUT."

You know what I'd do? I'd get out.

But there's always that family that decides it just *has* to stay: They scraped up all their life savings and finally paid the 30% deposit on this house, dammit. They didn't do anything wrong. They know their rights. So they'll get exorcists or try to move that ancient Indian burial ground underneath the house, or at least get Al Gore to bless the house as low in carbon emissions.

But in the end, does the house and the family in such a movie reach some sort of compromise, a *détente* of sorts? I'm still waiting for that ending.

*Dad at a barbecue in the backyard, talking with a friend: "Oh, yeah, our house USED to be haunted, but we've reached an understanding and we're all good now."*

Usually in the movies, the house just self-destructs; the family members and their dog barely make it out in time as they look on the fiery implosion of their would-be homestead. They thank God for saving their lives as they engage in a family group hug. Sure, they lost the house and everything they had in it, but hopefully mom and dad were sensible and got haunted house insurance.

The point is simple: You don't have to fight with an illogical system that doesn't want to have anything to do with you. You're not a prisoner of your school, and there's no lock on the door keeping you in.

So just open the door … and walk out.

In so many of my discussions with parents, some of whom want to sue or otherwise fight the status quo, I hear and see fear. It's part of the reason why they don't want to take steps to make changes in their lives.

Remember this: It's always easier to just go with the flow, especially when nothing seems to change in any dramatic way on a day-to-day basis. Most parents fear change. They fear they don't know where or how to start.

Fear will paralyze you and make you make awful decisions. The ultimate in such awful decisions is doing nothing, accepting the status quo. But you *must* take action, now. Not next year, next month, or even next week. You must start *right now*. There are some who know how—by gathering together and having like minds, like the soccer mom PTA members consisting of Jews, Christians, Asians, Indians, Koreans who successfully pushed back against the California LGBTQ+ teaching mandate. But those pushbacks are rare and require total commitment among similarly minded parents.

Wokism is a cancer. And like cancer, you must take the thankfully relatively minor steps now to stop it from metastasizing later. You either make those changes and experience a little discomfort now or do nothing and pay for it dearly later. Whatever discomfort in adjustments your kids might go through now, it'll be nothing compared to the contempt and hate you'll get in the years to come.

Simply put: Pay a bit now, or pay a *lot* later.

## CHAPTER III

# WHAT *WILL* WORK

To understand what *will* work, we must understand what actually motivates children, what they yearn for. In the most basic terms, they need purpose and passion. You need to *show* them what you believe, and why. Then it needs to be part of your daily lives. Give that to them, and you'll be more than halfway there.

## Purpose and Passion

One of the few moments in the original *Star Wars* trilogy (episodes 4, 5 and 6—the better ones) people rarely discuss is when Yoda trains young, immature and impetuous Luke as a Jedi knight. While training him on the planet Dagoba, Yoda yammers on endlessly to Luke about the Dark Side of the Force, all with his insufferable backwards grammar. (Why is communicating so hard for Yoda, by the way? It's so straightforward: Subject, verb, predicate... Subject, verb, predicate.)

At one point during his training, Luke senses his friends Hans Solo and Princess Leia are in grave danger, and he resolves to help them. He must go, he tells Yoda. But Yoda is strongly against it. Why? Because Luke's training is not yet complete. Without complete training, Yoda knows Luke will be susceptible to succumbing to the Dark Side, just like you-know-who. And that just did not work out well with that guy.

Luke shrugs it off and goes anyway. Thanks for all the cool mind tricks, Luke seems to say, but he's got this now. But almost as if Yoda could have predicted it, Luke faces temptation when poppa later offers Luke to rule the galaxy with him, "as father and son." To sweeten the offer, Dad assures Luke that "Vader & Son" will be on the letterhead of all future galaxy correspondence.

But Luke resists, tells Dad he will "never be like" him (which, no matter how tough Vader thought he was, had to sting at least a little), and goes on to save his buddies. The rebellion lives to fight another day in a not-as-good-but-still-fun *Return of the Jedi*.

So it all worked out. But the risk was high. To make sure he would never waver into the dark side of the Force, Luke should have stuck to the training and seen it through.

There's a lesson in all this: You can't do goodness half-assed. You're up against some powerful purveyors of passionate persuasion. If you don't show your kids you passionately care about America, God, and the fight against evil, they'll assume it's not so important to you.

Kids crave purpose, and they want to see *passion* in that purpose. Contrary to the self-centered beginnings of their lives, they quickly want to know there are important things beyond themselves. Kids instinctively *want* to love their country, to be on the winning "team," to be one of the Good Guys. More importantly, they want to believe in a higher being that loves them, protects them, and who is in charge of everything.

So, help them along. Work with these instincts and needs. Embrace them and encourage them. Teach them those things, and teach them with passion. They'll *want* to absorb and share your passion.

Because if you don't, there are plenty of Darth Vaders who will step in to give them that passion. It may be a passion for everything you're against, but passion is passion.

Think of it like when you're really thirsty: If you're desperate enough, you'll drink almost anything in front of you. Even if it's Kool-Aid.

## Understanding Plasticity, or "First In, Wins"

When I was in fourth grade, our art teacher had us make little statuettes out of clay. It was so fun to play with that moist, soft and malleable stuff. It seemed you could make anything that came to mind. She encouraged the kids to make clay head figures with silly faces, and that's what we all did. I made my own, thought it was okay, and left for the day. I didn't much like what I had started but figured I'd finish up the next day.

The problem with clay is that, if you leave it exposed to outside air for too long, it starts to harden. You can soften it up again with a small amount of water, but the longer you wait, the more water and more effort you'll need to be able to soften it up again for shaping purposes.

What I didn't know was that the art teacher had fired up all our clay figures in the kiln that evening, and glazed them over with what we had each told her were our favorite colors.

When I came into the classroom the next day, I was very upset. My head figure, which was supposed to be a silly man with a big nose, big ears, and wide smile, suddenly looked wildly different. The glaze had made it look ghoulish, even scary. I don't know quite how, but the dark green color of the glaze had transformed it into something hideous. I hated it.

On the other hand, the art teacher could not have been more thrilled. "Now you can each take your masterpieces home!" she exclaimed to all of us.

I eventually got up the courage to tell her I hadn't quite finished my head figure and asked if I could still change it. She said she was sorry but explained once it was glazed, it was permanent.

My mom picked me up from school and I went home, a bit sullen. My mom kept complimenting me on my great project—which I figured is what moms were supposed to do. I kept looking down at it on my lap the whole ride home. I kept trying to will myself to like it.

Later that night, I put it on my desk in the bedroom, and eventually went to bed. When I turned off the light, I still could see its darkened shape. It scared the crap out of me.

Eventually I got up and put it up in the upper shelf of my sliding door closet, behind some clothes, and then slid the closet door shut. I just didn't want to see it. For that matter, I wished it didn't exist. Still, I knew it was there all night, this monster of my own creation. And if I went to sleep, it might get out of the closet and kill me.

Over the months, I forgot about it. Eventually, however, my mom was cleaning out the closet and some clothes pulled it along with it. It fell to the floor and it broke into several pieces. My mom was so apologetic. I just sat there as she told me about it down in the kitchen. I remembered the monster of course, but I was glad for its demise.

"Can I go out and play now?" I asked. She nodded her head. I imagine in her mind she figured this was my way of processing my great loss. If she didn't handle this fragile moment just so, this could be a traumatic event I might bring up in therapy sessions for decades to come.

Plasticity. It's the concept that kids are incredibly flexible in how they learn. As famous child psychologist Jean Piaget put it, children are engaged in a constant effort to make sense of their world through a process of assimilation, accommodation, and equilibration. Each child develops "schemas," like index cards, that he or she uses to process and file information in their brains as they learn. With each new bit of information, they reshape their understanding of the world.[12]

Infants are born with an overabundance of synapses, or connections between neurons. These are the most fundamental parts of our brains. As infants gain more experience with the world, time prunes their synapses down, leaving only the ones they actually use. Most scientists studying the mind believe there is a special window of time when a child's brain is especially receptive to learning language.[13] There is a reason why we refer to young kids' minds as "sponges:" It's like we put them in a bath, and they absorb whatever liquid we soak them in.

This "sponge" analogy extends to everything else they absorb: Curiosity, skepticism, math, logical reasoning, courage, and its corresponding sense of risk-taking. It extends to perspective, sharing, work, sacrifice, community, happiness and gratitude (or lack thereof). It likely extends to virtually everything he learns.

And more important than anything is this one simple fact: First in, wins.

Draw from your own experience: when you hear a song you've heard many times before, your mind tends to drift to where you heard it the first time: perhaps in your car, at a party, wherever. Your brain forever "locks" that song to that moment and location. For me, for example, I remember where I first heard *Band on the Run*, by Paul McCartney. My mom was driving me back home from a little league baseball game, and I saw the sun set as we were driving west on Putnam Road in Cos Cob, Connecticut.

Think also of how you seem to like the first version of a song you hear, or even a whole play. Example: when the hit Broadway play *Hamilton* came out, I listened to it first on Apple Music, over and over again with my kids. I then took them to see the Los Angeles version at the Pantages theatre. It seemed to pale in comparison. By contrast, one of my good friends felt exactly the opposite: Discovering it *first* at the Pantages theatre, and then wanting to hear it with her kids later in Apple Music. She felt the original Apple Music version was lacking.

First in, wins. And the same is generally true for philosophy, religious outlook, musical preferences—or ideas.

For decades now, the Left has known all such things, gunning to influence your children at as young an age as they can. Oh, they'll let you go to the hospital to give birth to your baby and hug your new bundle of joy. You can have all your dreams of playing catch or taking her to ballet or violin lessons. You can dream all you want about how he's going to be a true (fill in your alma mater and its corresponding mascot). You can change his diapers and help your kid learn to ride a bike.

But sooner than you know it, they'll be itching to tap into your kids' lives. They'll start making comments through their nursery teachers, kindergarten teachers, and beyond. They know we parents rarely have stay-at-home moms, and dads are more absent than ever. For the dads who do remain in the family, they're chasing business deals and working just to make whatever they can to make ends meet.

The left knows another thing: people are going to church far less often. Why should they? Who wants to squander their precious weekend relaxing time getting dressed, driving to church, and then being "on" and reading out loud boring scriptures? Plus you could be making money: Don't forget how expensive college is going to be for little Stephanie one day.

But the church was the primary venue for meaning for most families. It was also the weekly opportunity for dads to echo the values the church spoke about that day. Now that's gone. Along with it, there's little community service or discussion about how to help others.

Families rarely have dinner together. Home has become a mere central meeting place where related people go to get food, get their laundry done, and prepare for activities elsewhere.

The Left knows you don't have time to involve yourself in your kids' lives, sports, or friends. Likewise, parents have essentially abandoned any interest in schools. The result? Unacceptably poor education where kids know little to nothing of what they should. Unions have taken over, advancing only the interests of teachers and progressive agents who keep inserting one Woke agenda item after the other.

As the late Steve Jobs, the iconic founder of Apple put it: "The problem … is that parents went away. [They] stopped paying attention to their schools… Mothers started working and they didn't have time to spend at PTA meetings and watching their kids' school. … Parents spent less and less time involved in their kids' education."[14]

Jobs was bemoaning the loss of educational rigor and substance. It was a fair thing to bemoan, but it was all due principally to parents' retreat from their kids' lives. They had ceded ground to educators.

Parents figured teachers and administrators surely have the kids' best interests in mind. To them, it was kind of like dealing with the plumber, electrician, pool guy, or gardener: You nod your head as they tell you their recommendations for fixing that leak or wiring issue, but you have little idea what they're talking about. You want to sound intelligent, so you fake it and at some point you say something like: "Well, that's exactly what I was thinking. Let's do that. I'm sure you'll handle it right." You quickly conclude your little pow-wow, because frankly you'd rather do anything else in your very busy life. They're the experts, after all, and you don't second guess them.

That's the way it's become with the schools. You have no idea which grade they start teaching fractions, decimals, or Indian I mean Native American history. As they get older, you realize that you forgot all about chromosomes, quadratic equations or how to divide fractions. You don't know when the Constitution was ratified, or just how the American Independence War actually ended (but then you heard the soundtrack from *Hamilton*, and now you're all good at least on that front).

So, like you hired the plumber and electrician and went along with their suggestions, you "hired" your kids' educators, either directly through private school, or indirectly through your tax dollars.

But there's a distinct difference here: We rarely would leave plumbers, electricians, or the HVAC guys alone in our house with our jewelry or other valuables—and certainly not alone with our young kids. In the back of our mind, we think it's only sensible they know we're there. We wouldn't want to come home to realize that jewelry, cash or credit cards were missing. At least we're actually *there*.

But with our educators, we leave our kids alone with them — for hours a day, week after week. And they raid your kid, as it were. They're like hoodlums ransacking through your home, thrilled like kids in a candy store for these incredibly easy pickings. And you were the ones who just brought them.

No, it's worse than that: When it comes to the kids' minds, you actually delivered the loot *to* them. You even saved them the trouble of traveling to your house to loot it. You're like a bank sending a truck to deliver those money sacks with the big dollar signs on them *to* the robbers' homes.

And the looting continues in college. Take the example of Annabella Rockwell who attended Mount Holyoke College in Massachusetts starting in 2011. Mount Holyoke is an all-female "elite" liberal college that left the young woman "totally indoctrinated" and estranged from the parents who raised her. Her parents paid $60,000 a year for that honor. After graduation, her mother would have to pay a $300-a-day "deprogrammer" to undo all the brainwashing.

It took years, but it worked. As Annabella put it herself: "I [had seen] everything through the lens of oppression and bias and victimhood. I came to the school as someone who saw everyone equally. I left looking for injustice wherever I could and automatically assuming that all White men were sexist. My thoughts were no longer my own."

The college had encouraged a "MoHo chop," an initiation ritual designed to abandon gender roles by cutting one's hair. By her junior year, however, Rockwell noticed a shift in herself after taking a gender studies class.

"I was told there's the patriarchy, and … [y]ou've been oppressed, and you didn't even know it. Now you have to fight it. And I just went down this deep rabbit hole." Her professors actively encouraged her to alienate herself from her parents. They even offered their homes to stay in, especially during the holidays. If you didn't believe "this stuff," the college and your fellow students would ostracize you.

Her mom, Melinda Rockwell, said it was like walking a tight-rope: "I couldn't push too hard or I'd lose her, but if I let go, I felt I might not see her again. It was as bad as trying to get a child off the streets who's on heroin. Everyone is so sure it won't happen to their child. But it will. [Professors and older students] tell the students they are special ... then they tell them how oppressed they are and what victims they are and how they have to go out in the world and be activists to stop the oppression."

Another former Mount Holyoke College student, 29-year-old [now] conservative activist Laura Loomer said that she left after just one semester freshman year due to bullying: "The entire culture there revolved around hating men and being a lesbian," Loomer said. As she put it, Mount Holyoke and all the Seven Sisters have become centers for indoctrination: "It's a bastardization of higher education ... for the sake of advancing a toxic agenda."[15]

Annabella Rockwell, who worked for Hillary Clinton's 2016 presidential campaign after graduating with a history degree, credited her mother's "relentlessness." She said if it wasn't for her mom's "harping at me and never giving up," she'd probably still be living in Massachusetts, working for some super-progressive politician, hanging out with people I had nothing in common with except ideology and drinking all the time. "And I'd be miserable," she said.

She said that her views began to change during the 2020 George Floyd protests, when she saw so much hypocrisy flowing from the event.[16]

Wow. 2020. Assuming the indoctrination began early in 2011 when she first matriculated, that means it took hold of her for almost *nine years.* And her mother was fighting it for most of that time.

300 bucks a day for say, at least five years. You do the math. If you can't or won't, let me help you with this: Even if you discount for every weekend, sick day, and holiday, it's actually far more than the four years of tuition combined.

It's not the parents' fault, of course, but I always think how these parents must feel: That they delivered their own children *to* these abusers. *Why did I deliver little Jack to these monsters? Why didn't I see the signs? How will I ever forgive myself?* It must play over and over in their heads, an infinite loop of guilt, to rationalizing, to guilt again.

One of the best ways to understand the changes in your own country is by seeing it through the eyes of immigrants who have recently come here. To them, it's a shock to hear such hatred of America, when they had heard nothing but how wonderful America was for all their lives.

Even defectors from totalitarian countries such as North Korea can't believe what universities are teaching students. Take Yeonmi Park, a brave woman who had a harrowing escape from North Korea to ultimately come to America and attend Columbia University. She was dismayed to see what American professors were teaching: "I realized, 'Wow, this is insane.' I thought America was different, but I saw so many similarities to what I saw in North Korea that I started worrying."

One professor scolded her when she expressed a love for Jane Austen novels (those are colonialist and racist). Park found it bizarre that professors asked students what their pronouns were. "Even North Korea is not this nuts. North Korea is pretty crazy, but not *this* crazy," she added.

Park said her experience at Columbia made her believe that American students were losing the ability to think critically, something she said she is all too familiar with from her time in North Korea.[17]

We need to be vigilant, more so now than ever. We need to understand education centers have become *cults*. Before you grimace, consider what all cults have in common:

(1) *Alienation and isolation.* Cults separate their target from your parents, your family, and your friends. This helps fulfill the mind control aspirations of the leader and also creates a "hive" mind between the new person and other members.

(2) *Encouraging total dependency.* People in the cult must feel incapable of living an individual life outside the norms of the group.

(3) *Extreme beliefs.* Cult members hold to dogmatic, extreme, and almost always bizarrely irrational beliefs. Further, they can't question these beliefs without fear of some sort of smack down from the leader or other group members.

(4) *Veneration of a single individual or rallying cry.* While there may not be one particular individual advancing this particular "cult" (although I suspect one day there will be) there are certainly groups and experts that embrace—without any deviation—social justice issues such as transgenderism, patriarchy, colonialism, etc., that require total allegiance to the cause. There is no "gray" area or nuance accepted.[18]

(5) *Money, time, and the altering of normal behavior.* Mount Holyoke's strong encouragement to girls to cut off their hair in their first year is just a mild form of this. Many cults demand that you deliver your money and assets (sometimes all of it) and certainly your time. In some cases, they expect you to perform acts that you would never consider (example: sending hate mail to your parents, women allowing themselves to be part of a harem of the cult leader, or straight men reluctantly engaging in homosexual sex as "proof" of their loyalty, as happened in the Jim Jones cult in Guyana of the late seventies).

(6) *Being "one" with a group, a sense of euphoric belonging, and purpose.* This may be the most significant factor: Every human being craves purpose and a need to belong. This is the *primary* offering of all cults. *Join us, and we will accept you.* This factor may be the easiest one in a world where parents give their children little to belong to. Certainly, there is very little teaching of the importance of being an American. There is even less talk about the community that faith would bring, let alone God.

In short, far from educational institutions having mere commonalties with cults, they have become cults *par excellence.*

We are sending our kids to institutions that exploit and abuse our kids, but in a different way: They molest their minds, shaping them into something we would never imagine: A hater of faith and God, America, family and all things you otherwise hold dear. They flip your child from the inside out, like in that horror story "The Dark," where a fog inverts the body like a hand taking off a wet rubber glove ("Skin on the inside...raw flesh on the outside! His organs just...hanging...").

It may be imperceptible from a day-to-day perspective, but after enough time it dawns upon you: She's changed. She's somebody else now. She's been... altered.

And as the clay of your kids' mind hardens, the more water it will take to soften that clay and bring your child back. Just ask Melinda Rockwell about that.

And God forbid your child gets the glaze.

# CHAPTER IV

# THE FOUR STEPS

The good news is that you can prevent all of this. And it's not that much of a challenge. It takes vigilance, yes, but it won't cripple you emotionally or financially. Nor will it suck all the time out of your lives.

In summary, I'll break it down to these four basic principles:

1. Plan for it
2. Get ahead of it
3. Explain it
4. Laugh at it and dismiss it.

Each of these steps build upon the other, and each of them reinforces the other. You must get ahead of each of the issues that concern you. Then, once you can explain to your child the madness of what's going on around them, and appeal to their natural sense of *damn-that's-just-crazy*, you're more than eighty percent of the way there.

# Plan for It (and Plan on It)

*"The education of all children, from the moment that they can get along without a mother's care, shall be in state institutions."*

— Karl Marx

We know that leftist ideology seeks to get into your child's brain at earlier and earlier ages. Karl Marx knew as much and would be ever so proud of his leftist proteges doing his bidding today.

Although in previous generations schools traditionally discussed sex very lightly in fifth grade and then developed more fully in sixth grade, sex education is now reaching further into the lower grades—fourth graders have contests about who can put the condom on the banana fastest.[19]

Even in advertising, they encourage sexuality for kids, even with otherwise cuddly bears. In one photo advertising campaign from Balenciaga, a child holds a teddy bear, in "bondage" chains. In the same photo compilation, it included a seemingly "hidden" court document about virtual child porn. What was that document? An excerpt from the US Supreme Court opinion in *United States v. Williams*, upholding part of a federal child pornography law. The good news was that the head designer of Balenciaga was quick to acknowledge that "it was inappropriate to have kids promote objects that had nothing to do with them." So all better.

Wait … *that* was what was wrong with it? It was just a bad marketing choice, like advertising extreme mountain biking adventures in AARP magazine? Also, he "never ha[d] an intention" of advocating child sexual abuse.[20] In other words, it's not what it looks like and shame on us all for not knowing his true, innocent, intentions. Quick query, though: just what *were* your intentions? Still confused.

Three-year-olds have "drag queen story hour," where men dressed and made-up outlandishly as women sit and read simple children's books to them.[21] *Why is this a thing, you wonder to yourself. What positive experience can my child gain from hearing a story from a drag queen? Why not have stories read by fireman, dentists, or freemasons? Is there some sort of important association between stories and drag queens that I'm missing?*

Put simply: Just whom is "drag queen story hour" benefitting? It's not entirely clear, but it certainly isn't your child. Advocates argue it helps avoid the "heteronormative" imposition upon children. The idea is to "instill the imagination and play of gender fluidity of childhood and gives kids glamorous, positive, and unabashedly queer role models."[22]

Studies show that children don't meaningfully understand the distinction between boys and girls until they're about three and a half.[23] Yet here they are at that critical developmental stage in their lives, watching men preen and prance as women. This can't be good: you figure the experience messes the kids' minds one way or another.

Think that observation is ridiculously anecdotal, and that one can't meaningfully draw any conclusions from it? It's prevalent in far more cities and towns throughout America than you might imagine. It's actually a thing—one that appears to be orchestrated in time and scope. The question is why.

You don't even have to have drag queen story hour, or sexually explicit picture books in the elementary school library, to know that something is up. Teachers nationwide are on a warpath to make sure your kids know that being a boy or a girl is a question of how one feels about himself, as easily changed as the clothes they might wear for the day. *You don't have to be a boy or girl. We want you to know that. You can be anything you want. This is America!* Well, they probably wouldn't add that last part, what with suggesting America might be awesome.

And if you clamor to remove the pornographic books out, you are against free speech. Worse, you're "silencing" certain voices. It's not clear what those certain voices are, except perhaps the prurient voices in one's head. Or perhaps they're talking about pedophiles, and they believe pedophiles have the right to have your child see their pornography.

They're obsessed with this mission. And if you suggest your child is, in fact, a boy (what with him having a penis and all), they will dismiss you as a Neanderthal—no offense to Neanderthals. You are malignantly presumptuous. *You* are what's wrong with America.

You can be sure about one thing: This *will* happen. The teachers await your child's class and can't wait to *not* address the kids as "boys and girls." They're going to make a point of demonizing any assumptions about distinctions between anyone, at least in the world of gender. They're happy to make distinctions between and among black, Hispanic, and white, and even sexual preferences. But not gender. With gender, they're happy to put everyone into one big blender and hit "frappé."

And they just *can't wait* to ask each child whether he/she is a boy or a girl, and what their favorite pronouns are—even before they know what a "pronoun" is. You hope the conversation might go something like this:

*Teacher: So tell me, young Johnny, what pronouns do you prefer to be called?*

*Johnny: What's a pronoun?*

*Teacher, muttering to herself: Damn, this is going to be harder than I thought.*

In your dreams, if they ask something like this, you hope your boy will retort something like: "Seriously, you can't figure out if I'm a boy or girl? Are you like one of those stupid people?" But alas, they're just too young.

There's the rub, I suppose. That's exactly what they're counting on.

The point of it all is planning for it, since we know this will almost certainly happen in public schools and many non-parochial private schools. It'll happen in your child's camps and extra-curricular events, even at the local YMCA. It'll seep in through social media apps and most of your kids' favorite shows on TV.

But think of all the things you do plan for: you insure your house, car, and health for the inevitable accidents and diseases which might befall you. You save for your child's college fund. You plan your vacation, you don't just up and leave for the airport:

*Friend 1: Hey, Charlie, where are you going on vacation?*

*Friend 2: I figure the missus and I will go to the airport and we'll get on some plane that'll take us somewhere.*

*Friend 1: That's a capital idea, Charlie. You really know how to live.*

For that matter, people generally don't stumble into their weddings:

*Susie: Hey, Bernadine, I heard you're getting married! When is your wedding?*

*Bernadine: We just set it yesterday! It'll be tomorrow. We're going to have hundreds of our friends show up. We'll have it some big place, I think. Like maybe a church or synagogue—one of those kind of places. I figure we'll have some religious guy show up and say stuff to us to make it official and everything. Caterers will come and feed us and we'll have some cake at the end of it.*

*Susie: Wow, tomorrow? What time?*

*Bernadine: Sometime during tomorrow.*

*Susie: (giddy and clapping her hands in joy for her friend): That's so exciting!*

Governments should plan for war, too:

*Chairman of the Joint Chiefs of Staff: Sir, it looks like the Russians, the Chinese, and the Iranians have gathered forces and are heading our way from every direction. They say they're going to burn everything to the ground. Or we think they said words to that effect—we don't have very good translators.*

*President: Good God… So I take it you'll send off our battleships and destroyers and scramble our jetfighters and gather up all our infantry and such?*

*Joint Chief of Staff: That's not a bad idea. We should probably get some of those things.*

You get the point. We seemingly plan for everything else — home security, pool maintenance, dental visits, car maintenance, savings plans for college, Passover, Thanksgiving and Christmas get-togethers. We even plan on how best to get our kids into the best nursery school (and then elementary, middle school, and high school).

But many parents have no game plan for the inevitable raid of their children's brains. Yet it's coming.

What's your plan to guard your child's mind, knowing the infiltrators are coming for them? You can't be naïve enough to think it'll never happen to your little Aiden or Penelope or Bella.

And if you don't plan *for* it—and plan *on* it—you'll be helpless. This is no different than not having a plan to talk to the kids about peer pressure, cigarette smoking, alcohol or drugs, and then expecting your little darling to not smoke, drink or take drugs. This is no different than not talking to your kids about being smart about sex and the possible ramifications of pregnancy and disease. This is no different than handing the kids a key to your car and never talking to them about driving carefully.

*Mother: Oh dear Husband, I just saw our thirteen-year-old-son Kevin take the keys to our car and drive off. He was loading it up beforehand with several six-packs of beer, and several bags of marijuana. Also, he was texting on his phone while he was reversing the car into the busy street.*

*Father: (putting his arms comfortingly around her shoulders): Come now, good wife. He'll figure this stuff out. It'll all be fine.*

Absurd as this scenario appears, it is *exactly* what you're doing when it comes to the inevitable raid of your child's mind. Unless you have a *system* in place to guard against it ahead of time, your kid might as well be riding with Kevin.

Don't pretend it won't happen. Plan on the issues coming up. Then get ahead of it.

## Get Ahead of It

Your child will be facing serious threats from her own school—no less formidable than the threats of drugs, teenage sex, and alcohol. The only difference is that these threats will be coming directly from her own teachers and other faculty.

While it's important to know that it's coming, you'll have to actually talk specifics about the impending raid. You may not have to call it out as a "raid" to your child, but it's very real.

Is it really that difficult to anticipate? You hear about it everywhere on the news and other media: transgender this, pronoun that, racism everywhere, America bad. American Indians perfect. Capitalism bad. Socialism good. Christianity and masculinity are toxic. Fossil fuel use, cow flatulence and even our own breathing will render our planet uninhabitable in 300 or so years. God is a fabrication to keep people in line. Evolution explains everything. Democrats save democracy, Republicans are fascists.

You know that at least some of the teachers in your child's school will push exactly these things at some point in your child's education. They may not teach it all in one month, but remember they have thirteen years to get into your kid's mind and ransack it (more if you include pre-kindergarten). And that's *before* your kid goes to college, where erudite and noble leftists in offices with a poster on the wall reading "Bring back the trains!" next to a copy of the Andy Warhol painting of Mao hope to isolate your kid even further and appeal to an idealism and sense of belonging that you may never have given them.

So if you know it, then *get ahead of it.* Start talking to your kids early on about God, America's greatness and why capitalism has created the greatest advances in the history of civilization, the gifts of Judaism and Christianity, and so on.

How early? As soon as they are able to absorb information. See an American flag? Rejoice at it with your kid as you pass by and say how cool that family in the house must be because they obviously love America. Talk to your kids about everything and anything from the Bible and the history of America — from the courage of King David against Goliath to how George Washington outsmarted the British in Manhattan, Trenton and Yorktown.

Then talk to them about God and tell them about the extraordinary improbabilities that life, the world and the universe could come about randomly. Smirk at the idea that it could all happen by itself.

Talk every moment that you can. You'll have fun in the process. Present the arguments of the other side and then show their weaknesses and mock it. It won't be hard. Best of all, I promise it will be *fun.*

You may have to educate yourself about the facts and the theories of the other side, but it won't be a serious challenge. And the guidelines of this book will provide great pointers for resources and methods of communication with your child.

## Is this Indoctrination? Yes, and You Better Get to It

You may say that all this is a form of indoctrination of your own kids, and I'm advocating exactly the same thing I'm decrying about social media, entertainment, and the schools. I have three responses to this argument:

### You're the Boss, They're Not

First, despite their glorified perception of their roles, schools and teachers are *not* on equal footing in the raising of kids department. Let's be clear: while kids can experience many influences, parents have the primary role to shape and mold their kids in the way they see fit. Only parents know and care about their kids deeply in the way they do. It is parents who have ongoing obligations and care for their kids, legally, morally, and socially.

Parents gave birth to the kids, fed them, changed diapers, scheduled and attended doctor visits, sports and school activities, made sure they were doing their homework, dealt with discipline and chores and monsters under the bed. Parents are the ones paying out of their behinds for it all, too. Parents advocate for their kids and read to them, help them with their lemonade stand, teach them to ride a bike and deal with bullies.

Parenting is a full-time job. By contrast, a teacher will be in your child's life for nine or so months, and then only during school hours—not night times, weekends, holidays, or school breaks. Then she moves on to the next academic year with a whole crop of different faces she doesn't know (but will soon refer to as "her" kids).

By contrast, parents will be parents from the birth of their kids to the end of their lives. Hopefully their children will feel and remember that parenting even after the parents die and echo their parents' values to their own kids.

In short, teachers are *not* on the same footing as parents, not be a longshot. Any claim to the contrary is maddeningly out of whack with basic reality.

But claim it they will. Here's an infamous (and ominous) tweet from Randy Weingarten, head of the NEA, in response to parents' complaining about what the schools are teaching their kids: "Educators love their students and know better than anyone what they need to learn and to thrive."

Let me repeat that in case you missed it: *Teachers know better than anyone else what is best for your kids.*

Betsy DeVos, the former Education Secretary, immediately responded: "You misspelled parents." It was a brilliant response—and absolutely spot on. But her response were just words from a former Education Secretary. They can do little to fight the savage horrible Weingarten *zeitgeist*. And *zeitgeist* it is: Weingarten's post wasn't a one-off quirky statement which a high-ranking official let slip, say in a "hot mic" moment. She really believed it.

Former Virginia governor Terry McAuliffe had also echoed Weingarten's "we got this, you don't" attitude in 2021: "I don't think parents should be telling schools what they should teach." McAuliffe then lost the governorship in a dramatic election loss to Glen Youngkin, in significant part because of this statement.

This attitude went all the way to President Biden, who dotingly quoted a teacher who proclaimed: "There's no such thing as someone else's child. Our nation's children are *all* our children." He went on to say that teachers "hold the kite strings" of our children's future, and they "are determining our future."[24] No mention of parents or family holding those kite strings. Parents are just secondary characters, like Newman or Puddy on *Seinfeld*.

This is the audacity, the hubris, even the sense of arrogant entitlement which shape the teachers' following attitudes about themselves and your kids: *You are simple people. We will save you from yourselves. We're the experts. Thank God for us. Your kids belong to us.*

No they don't. Remember that.

## Find Your Inner Israeli

Second, they're going to try to indoctrinate your kids, so you've got to anticipate it and fight back ahead of time with your own indoctrination. It's a battle for your kids' minds, and if you don't recognize it as a battle, you *will* lose it.

So you'll need to shore up your fortress, get ready for the slings, arrows, bullets and hot black tar they're going to launch at you. Prepare for the digging under the fortress walls and their secret underground tunnels.

You'll have to think of yourself like you're Israel, that small country in the middle east which must constantly deal with terrorist groups and hostile neighboring countries, day after day, hour after hour. But Israel knows all the best infrastructure and defensive planning still won't ever work unless it educates their citizens, practically from birth, instilling in them the necessity of constant vigilance, planning for the ever-present possibility of war, infiltration, and sneak attacks. Israelis are *always* contemplating how the enemy will attack next. They're rarely reactive; they usually know the attacks are coming well before the enemy attempts them. And they always know who and where the enemy is.

And that's exactly how you need to prepare for the onslaught they're preparing against your child in his school and everywhere else.

Find your inner Israeli.

## Indoctrination Is Your Job, Not Theirs

Third, whether you accept it or not, indoctrination is what parents *do*. We give them religion (or not). We give them a sense of duty for country (or not). We navigate them in the world of sports, art, humor, travel, hobbies, music and even entertainment. We tell them what's right and wrong, and what is silly and not worth pursuing. We give our take on politics, family, global warming, transgenderism, evolution, and history. We tell them how to view the outside world. We may even raise them kosher or vegan (both as I do with my kids). We expect parents to do all these things. In fact, if we *don't* instill these things, we might very well be considered bad parents.

In short, we already shape their world—heavily. Yes, we even indoctrinate them. And you know something? Considering all the loss of sleep, diaper-changing, doctors' visits, reading to them, money spent on toys, tuition and teeth, time lost, the constant worrying, and self-doubt about your own abilities to parent at all—to say nothing of the potential liability for not raising your kids correctly (whatever "correctly" means), you shouldn't feel guilty about it at all. Parents are entitled to shape—even indoctrinate--their kids the way they see fit.

So is this indoctrination? You bet. Shed whatever distaste you may have with that word, and get to it.

## *The Good News*

Here's the good news: Once you realize *you* are responsible for how they navigate the world, once you realize you're at war with vicious outside forces who want to kidnap your kids' minds, and once you realize that you have to get to your kids before they do; it's actually easy.

You have the advantage of the home turf of their minds. You have the advantage of time and being first in your kids' minds. You also have the advantage of kids looking up to you, craving your approval, seeking purpose and boundaries, and wanting to figure out the world.

*You* are the first source for all those things. If you are not cultivating these needs early, you are failing in your most precious and important role—to shape and mold your kids into the great humans and contributors to civilization you know they can be.

If you wait to their teenage years, or even if you wait until they're ten or eleven, it'll be much, much harder. So start early—as early as your child can speak and comprehend what you say.

To boil it down to a simple phrase: Get ahead of it, and do it as soon as you can.

# Explain It

It's great to know what's coming. It's great even to get ahead of it. But it's not enough to say you're a believer in God. It's not enough even to say how awesome America is or how conservatism is better than whatever the progressives are selling. Too many conservative parents today just phone it in:

*Child: Daddy, which is better, the Republican Party or the Democrat Party?*
*Dad: The Republican party.*
*Child: Which religion is best?*
*Dad: Ours.*
*Child: Which country is the best?*
*Dad: America.*
*Child: Why are all those things the best?*
*Dad: 'Cause they just are.*
*Child: Okay.*
*Dad: Glad we had this talk, son... Oh, and don't do drugs.*

You have to get into the weeds of *why* it is so. You have to roll up your sleeves and see this as a long-term project. Think of it like the difference between *wanting* to build a house and actually *building* a house.

I may have had an advantage: I have almost never taken *anything* on faith alone—not God, America, nor capitalism. I always wanted to know *why* I should appreciate any of those things, let alone embrace them with passion.

I couldn't even accept Einstein's Law of Relativity (E = $mc^2$), or the Pythagoras formula on triangles ($a^2 + b^2 = c^2$) on faith. I needed to know just how those equations came to be. Even in my study of French, I always had to directly translate and deconstruct sentence fragments to get a comprehensive understanding.[*]

Likewise, I felt I should be able to articulate why I subscribed to my religion, my country, and my economic system. To do that, it meant I'd have to know logic, history, and human nature itself. In short, I needed to answer these basic questions: *Why do all we humans seem to have a yearning for a belief in a higher being? What were the major reasons for civilization? What system works best and why?*

---

[*] Example: *Est-ce que tu es ici?* does *not* mean "Are you here?" it actually means "Is it that you are here?"

Another way of putting it is, how did we get to where we are?

It helps if you have a natural interest in such matters. But even if you don't, you need to get interested. Find a way. Because your schools are very interested in such matters.

Remember what I wrote above about the WWII generation of soldiers coming home, who largely failed to explain the importance of Judeo-Christianity and America's greatness and goodness. It *was* understandable: Having seen the horrors of such a horrendous war, they wanted to just enjoy the benefits of America and start a family.

That came at a cost: their children, without the benefit of knowing basics of America and God, became aimless. They searched for meaning anyway and found it in social causes. Marxist and Marxist-lite teachers and professors were happy to fill the void.

We cannot repeat this massive mistake. Kids are in a constant search for meaning and purpose, just as adults are. It's imbedded within all of us. They need to love their country and their faith like a car needs fuel. Too many children today have a greater sense of loyalty to their favorite NBA or NFL team than they do to their country. For that matter, they might even have greater loyalty to their elementary school sports teams.

And team loyalty, as we all know, only lasts so long when everyone keeps drip-drip-dripping how bad you team is. Everyone wants to support a winner. You can only root for the Bad News Bears for so long.

And why *wouldn't* they abandon Team America? For many kids, they've heard little except hatred for America, that it's systemically racist, homophobic, transphobic, antisemitic, and anti-pedophile (that'll be the next thing, by the way). America invades other countries at the drop of a hat, throws its weight upon the rest of the world, exploits the resources and people of every other country, is obsessed with guns, can't seem to control its renegade and trigger-happy cops, and are generally arrogant and loud. Also, Americans eat *way* too much fast food. Come to think of it, America may very well be the worst country in the world.[25]

This is where we start. We talk to our kids about how America *is* great, how it became so, particularly how the world was before America. We show how America's revolution was the first revolution about an idea: Freedom. We show how America fought against slavery (that's right, through the Republican party, which was founded predominantly to fight slavery), and fought against later racism, which had been far more present everywhere else in the world, and still is.

We must talk about how America spread liberty, and because of that spread, America went from being the sole free country in the world at its founding, to being one of approximately 90 countries that are now described as "free" or "mostly free."[26]

We must talk about the innovations of America, not just through inventions (and there are an insane number of those, especially compared to inventions from any other country), but medical breakthroughs and discoveries, music and other entertainment, books, computers and the internet, clothing and fashion, and food.

And then say: "Isn't America *awesome*?"

*There's* your cause to be loyal to Team America. You start off with basic, irrefutable facts, and then get them to appreciate America. In fact, with my own kids, I came upon an idea after my youngest son wanted to play his usual game of going around the dinner table and naming all the characters of *the Simpsons* TV show. The idea was to go around and not repeat a character's name. If a person stumbles and can't think of a different character within five seconds, he or she loses the game.

Well, I got bored of that game after the say, twenty-seventh time we played it. But it dawned on me that we could do the same thing with American inventions, discoveries, and cultural innovations.* That game can seemingly last forever. Try it. You'd be amazed how suddenly appreciative your kid can be.

Likewise, we talk about God and how the world before monotheism was beyond brutal. We talk about how Judaism and Christianity created our sense of time, justice, truth, charity, the school system, hospitals, the scientific method and law and order.

And then we say: "Isn't it awesome to be Jewish/Christian?"

After that, we talk about what the left pushes: randomness and evolution as the sole explanation for our universe and our existence, and whether that makes sense; global warming/climate change and whether man can affect weather; how America is great because of free speech, but how the left wants to squash that; and finally the insanity of the claim that boys can be girls and vice versa.

And so much more.

We'll give specific talking points to make things easier, but the main point is this: talk as often as you can about America, God, and *why things are so*. Instill pride in all these matters because your child belongs to that heritage. Do it while you drive the kids in your car. Do it while you're waiting with your kid in line for the movies, at the dinner table and especially before they go to bed.** It appeals to their imagination, and to their sense of purpose, drive, loyalty, and, yes, pride.

Like I said: Kids are in a perpetual state of trying to make sense of their world. Help them along. Just put in the time. It's actually not hard, and you'll see how fun it can be as your kids

---

* Here are some major inventions to start with (more detail later on this): freedom, the car, the airplane, TV, the harnessing of electricity, the telephone, the internet, jazz, rock 'n roll, rap, personal computers, air conditioning, Uber, Airbnb, and all the original social networks. Countless inventions, discoveries, and other advances in the medical field. These are just a tiny fraction of America's contributions to the world. While other Western democracies have provided contributions as well (most notably Israel, whose contributions are beyond imagination considering its small size and lack of resources), it is fair to say there is no meaningful comparison.

** This should remind us of the Torah's commandment to teach one's children about God "…when you sit at home and when you walk along the road, when you lie down and when you get up." Deuteronomy 11:19. The Bible knows what it takes to keep your kids in the faith.

engage and ask questions and inject some ideas of their own. You'll share the ideas little David said earlier that day with your wife, and he'll beam with pride about it. As your kids engage, this will lead you to be more engaged. It'll be a self-reinforcing and self-perpetuating virtue cycle. You'll quickly realize you're on the right track.

Have fun in the game. And the best way to have fun while rejecting the progressive agenda? Laugh at it.

## Laugh At It and Dismiss It

*"I have never made but one prayer to God, a very short one: 'O Lord, make my enemies ridiculous.' And God granted it."*

— Voltaire

You've heard the advice many times: If you want to engage an audience, tell a joke or even a funny story about yourself before your speech. Ideally, you want the joke or story at least to nominally fit the main purpose of your speech.

People appreciate both stories and humor. Even under the most brutal of conditions, humor is often the most effective way to undermine tyrannical rulers. Example: two prisoners in a German concentration camp. One of them complains to the guard that he's found two flies in his soup rations. "This is an outrage!" says the other prisoner. "I only got one!"

Another of my favorites: In the former Soviet Union, where it was impossible to get basic services: A man goes to the government agency for communications to get a new phone. The services guy says, "The earliest date we have is five years from today." The man says: "Oh, okay. Can you make it in the afternoon?"

Surprised, the representative says, "What does it matter if it's in the afternoon? It's five years from now!"

The man responds: "Because my plumber is coming in the morning."

Attacking wokism head-on is important, but nothing works better than showing absurdities in today's new authoritarian-ism-with-a-smile culture. It has to be an instrumental part of your overall cocktail. In other words, don't just show that the leftists are wrong. Mock them.

As much as kids love to be proud of their country and religion, kids love absurdities. If you've ever played "opposite world" with your kids when they were little, you've seen this yourself. I did something very similar with my kids: When we saw something silly, I would say: "What's next? Horses riding people? Cars running on milk? Dogs walking their owners?" Let your kids add their own similar absurdities.

Once I was with my kids and we saw a crazy guy yelling in a supermarket. "Why is that man yelling, Daddy?" Response: "He thinks the government didn't give him enough cookies, and boy is he angry!"

They also understand the way the world *should* be, and they want a world of stability, where anything that flips that normative worldview is not only suspect, but silly.*

This part is almost too easy for us parents: I'll provide many examples later, but here are some obvious ones to play with:

*You: Can you believe it? Some schools are saying there's no such thing as boys and girls, and you can be either or nothing at all. Woohoo! I guess that means that goes for anything else! So I want to be a major NBA player now, and six-foot eleven. What about you, Charlie? What do you want to be?*

*Charlie: (ridiculous tone): I don't know, how about a space giraffe?*

*You: A space giraffe? Awesome! Why not? Anything goes in the land of the Left! Just think it and that's what you'll be. What a country!*

---

* At this point, I feel like I have to say what I'm *not* saying (because I have found my detractors like to claim I'm saying what I'm not saying). I am *not* saying that you should teach your children that anyone who is different from them is bad, stupid, or silly. Far from it: God makes everyone in all shapes, sizes, colors, and preferences. This is *not* about laughing at someone because he is gay, autistic, black, Hispanic, non-Christian, disabled, blind or deaf, or whatever. It *is* about not letting anyone cram untruths, absurdities, and impossibilities into your kids' heads.

Soon enough, they'll be saying they want to be Superman, Spiderman, Luke Skywalker, Napoleon, a flying turtle (yes, I heard that one; not quite clear on the allure of that one), or just plain invisible.

And to all those things you'll say: Sure! The appeal is all the more fun because you can morph into whatever you want on a daily or even hourly basis.

Work with this. Once you've given your kids permission to laugh at the left's absurdities (and remember—they're *all* absurd things), you'll be more than halfway to their full immunization. And you can tell your kids that when any administrator or teacher tells them absurdities at school, they should realize they're one of the silly people, teaching silly things.

Again, have fun with this. If you and your kids are not having fun while mocking it, then you haven't gone far enough.

Laughter is indeed the best medicine. It also happens to be the best weapon in your arsenal against the forces of evil.

Finally, wrap things up by *dismissing* the absurdities. Have them reach their own conclusions. This, too, is quite easy. You approach things by asking them what they think of certain crazy things, and what they would do. Examples:

*Scenario 1:*
*You: So, what do you think, Bobby? Do you think it's smart to make a law that says you can't have guns? What do you think would happen?*

*Bobby: Well, that's easy. Bad guys won't follow the rules. They'll keep their guns and good guys would not have guns. That would be dangerous for everyone.*

*You: I think that's a great point, Bobby. So what do you think of people who would tell you to get rid of all guns everywhere?*

*Bobby: That's just silly.*

And… scene….

*Scenario 2:*
You: *So, what do you think? Do you think there's no such thing as boys and girls? Just whatever you feel like being?*
Bobby: *Of course there are boys and girls.*
You: *I think that's spot on, Bobby. So what do you think of people who want to pretend there's no difference?*
Bobby: *That's just silly. It's so obvious.*
And ... Scene....

*Scenario 3:*
You: *So, what do you think? Do you think we shouldn't have police? Do you think we should instead have mental health workers to figure out what a criminals' feelings are?*
Bobby: *No. That's crazy. That wouldn't work.*
You: *Why not?*
Bobby: *Because bad guys don't listen unless they're afraid of guns.*
You (nodding): *Bobby, you sure make sense.*
And, ... Scene...

*Scenario 4:*
You: *So, what do you think? Is it fair for someone to get into a better school or get a better job because he's a minority, like black, Hispanic, or whatever? Even if he got bad grades or doesn't do any work at school?*
Bobby: *No. Of course not.*
You: *Why not?*
Bobby: *Because only people who do the best should get into the best schools and get the best jobs. It's like someone getting a trophy for being the fastest in the race, when he was the last. That wouldn't be right.*
You (nodding): *Bobby, that's such a good example.*
And, once again... Scene...

You might think these dialogue scenarios are too simplistic and obvious. And they are. But that's the beauty of it: they *should* be simplistic and obvious—especially to kids. They *should* play out exactly and as easily as I write above, *precisely* because they are so obvious.

Every kid knows that there's a difference between boys and girls. Every kid knows you can only stop bad guys with the threat of guns, and that guns protect people. Every kid knows it's not fair to penalize the successful just to avoid making someone else feel bad. Every kid should know that America is the greatest country in the world, that pure evolution makes no sense, and that God is real.

These *should* all be obvious, but what *you* think is obvious is not necessarily obvious to a kid. *They need to hear it from you.*

We parents as a group have failed to actually talk about these obvious matters with our kids. And because we haven't, the schools, media, and social media have swooped in and claimed the Field of the Obvious and planted their flag.

And then one day we realize these absurdities have become realities to our kids. Then we find ourselves scrambling to undo the madness—as did Melinda Rockwell at $300 a day for five or so years.

Talk to your kids. Appeal to their sense of basic understandings of what works, of common sense, and of the obvious. Appeal to their pride of being an American, Christian or Jew, and of being a boy or girl.

And do it as early as you can: the sooner they understand what *should* be obvious in their world, the stronger their resistance muscles will be to the woke madness later. Think of it like starting your kid off in a sport—the sooner he starts, the greater the muscle memory he'll develop for that sport. As every parent knows, at some point it gets too late to expect him to be a champion.

They'll understand it and thank you for helping make sense of the world around them. They'll laugh along with you at all those sillies who think that humans can change the climate, that you can become the opposite sex whenever you feel like it, or that you should get better grades, better treatment, or even massive reparations just on account of your skin color.[27]

But you *do* have to talk about it. Even if you think they already know it. It's your job.

One final note: notice how in every one of the scenarios above I start off with a question to the kid: "What do you think?" This is an important approach in the engagement of kids. It shows them respect for their input and thought process. It engages them while giving them an opportunity to obtain your approval. I highly recommend this approach, which is far more effective than simply telling them what to think.

# CHAPTER V

# HOW TO HANDLE THE HOT TOPICS

There are so many topics to tackle, from transgenderism to evolution to global warming. The following are just proposed ways to handle some of the key topics. These techniques have been quite effective with my own kids.

You know that these topics are going to crop up, sooner or later. Get ahead of them before the school and other outside influences do. In all of the topics, remember the four steps: identify the issue, get ahead of the issue, explain and then laugh at that issue. Finally, dismiss the leftist interpretation of the issue.

## Climate Change (formerly doing business as Global Warming)

This may be one of the most important issues to get your child to dismiss, and the sooner the better. Climate Change helps prop up many of the other canards, such as population control, America as a force for bad, socialism as a good thing, the unimportance of family and marriage, and the trivializing of sexuality and gender identity (all of which we will discuss separately, below).

So here goes.

## Identifying the Issue

The Left argues that our world is in a heap of trouble: Man-made global emissions will eventually cause a warming of the planet that will lead to the melting of Greenland and the polar ice caps, which will flood the shores of all earth's continents. Starvation will naturally ensue. Presumably we will resort to eating one another.

But there's good news: Eating each other will instantly solve the twin problems of hunger and our horrific overpopulation problem. Plus, we probably taste like chicken, so things won't really seem that different.

Never mind the alarmists want to divert trillions of dollars from solving actual world-wide problems (infectious disease, pollution, lack of education and clean water, etc.) to "fight" an unproven hypothetical future cataclysm.[28] Never mind also that they've been wrong on every doomsday prediction before—from Paul Ehrlich's *Population Bomb* scare, to lifeless oceans, to smog holocausts (both of which were to happen by no later than 1990, mind you). Never mind the big scare of the seventies and early eighties was global *cooling*.

*This* time they've got it right. But just in case, they really, really hope and ask you don't read all the stuff they predicted before. At least just don't bring it up.

*Man to woman who wants him to marry her: Honey, I'm just a little concerned. I learned recently that each of your five husbands before me were killed by slow-acting poison in their coffees and you inherited all their money.*

*Woman: I can't believe you're bringing that up. You must not love me. Now drink your latte and shut up.*

If you don't heed their warnings, then you hate the earth and are *very* short-sighted. Perhaps you're even a bit stupid. For sure, you're actually dangerous if you don't agree with them.

They're all for free speech, but let's face it: The Founding Fathers didn't intend for free speech to apply to existential things like this. So hold all the challenges, all you non-experts. The grown-ups have to put a pause on your freedoms and do some very important stuff to protect you from yourselves.

Sure, no one knows when the Great Apocalypse will happen. No one knows by how much the earth will warm, and no one knows if we can actually slow it down, let alone stop it or reverse it. No one appears to know by just how much the seas will rise (or when). Estimates seem to range the whole gamut from .36 of an *inch* to more than three *feet*[29], depending on the weather (if you will). Media outlets like CNN don't even give an estimate at all, providing only ominous mock-up photos imagining how various cities might look like underwater.[30]

What's that you say? That's not enough alarmism for you? All right, how about this: At least one global warming expert, Jason Box, predicts a possible rise by as much as *sixty-nine feet*.[31] He doesn't bother advising by just *when* that'll happen, but we can forgive that because the whole world drowning thing is an emergency, and in his rush to get the word out, he probably didn't have time to tell us.

Oh, and the estimates from NASA and other important government organizations keep accelerating upward every year. It's as if they noticed governments weren't listening to them enough, so our more informed elite betters needed to turn the alarmism up a notch. Think of it like increasing the electricity voltage on that torture victim who just ain't cooperatin'.

Also—and you would think this might be important—no one is quite sure what percent in the warming is due to man's activities, compared to natural forces at play which emit carbon and increase sea levels in spectacularly far greater amounts, such as solar flares, fluctuations in the moon's gravitational pull on tides, animal flatulence, and volcanic eruptions.[32] But the IPCC is happy to take a stab: they assure us that 97% of "scientists" (whatever that means) agree that humankind is responsible for the majority of climate warming. Indeed, "… humans are responsible for *more than* 100% of the global surface warming since 1950."[33] (Emphasis added).

Wait… *More* than 100%? For such great scientists, you'd think they'd understand math a bit better. Maybe it was for emphasis, like when people say they'd be "more than happy" to do something for you—a sort of "uber" happiness reflecting an ecstasy beyond your ordinary run-of-the-mill happiness.

Or maybe it's a new form of the "social justice" thing: A form of affirmative action like inflating grades for minority students or not arresting minorities for crimes because they've really had it rough for all those centuries. So you have to go the extra mile to make things right. To that end, it's only a matter of time before the 97% Guys tell us the Climate Change thing comes only from white male Christians, lest we make minorities feel bad.

But get all those out of your mind because none of those unresolved head-scratcher issues are important. The important thing is to do *something*, because computer models always know best—even if the models' estimate ranges are so large to render them meaningless, and even if humans input all the data into those models, and even if there are few if any standards to how people gauge, collect, and report temperatures.[34] And politicians, policymakers, and eco-activists are always objective and reach only the conclusions where science leads them.

Also, you would *think* climate researchers might be biased because research grants only go to those who advance climate change apocalypse theories. But you'd be very wrong. Because it's never about the money that's being thrown at them. It's about *truth*… even if they might profit from reaching the truth they're told to reach.

Next, governments and their leaders have made at best nonsensical overtures to "address" climate change. The so-called Paris Climate Change Accord (such a lofty title, it just *begs* respect) makes so many exceptions to "emerging" countries such as China and India that it can't possibly result in any meaningful stemming of the Great Apocalypse. It's like the old days when more than half of the plane or restaurant was a "smoking" section. Was there really a "non-smoking" section?

As it turns out, the world's "smoking" section today is pretty damn big and may be filled to capacity: China spews out more greenhouse gas than the entire developed world combined.[35]

Then there's the breathtaking hypocrisy of world leaders, who go to these very Climate Change summits in the very carbon-spewing private jets they claim are among the main contributors to the impending end of our planet, who drive fossil-fuel limousines and who own multiple mansions which each spew 21 times more carbon into the atmosphere than the average American home.[36] The only thing consistent about such leaders is how none of them ever address their hypocrisies, and how the media never calls them to account.

To my mind, the Climate Change hysterics achieved only one thing: Terrifying and instilling unnecessary fear, especially among children. If I were a ten-year old child today hearing my parents tell me of the oncoming flood (literally) that is going to wipe out the planet, I'd be peeing in my pants every night.

I'd have some questions, too, as I would lay curled up and rocking in my bed: *Why did my parents bring me into this world if I'm just going to drown in it? Why do so many people hate our planet? Why do they not care if I live?* I suppose also I would hate all those selfish people who didn't think like my parents.

But forget about the meaningless and questionable esti-mates, all the predictions that were wrong before, all those unresolved causation issues, the alarmism, unjustified fear tac-tics, and hypocrisies. Forget them all.

All you need do is look at their faces and puppy-dog eyes and see their passionate and indignant concern. They *must* be right.

But they're more like the bizarrely nasty Lucy from *Peanuts* fame, once again assuring poor innocent Charlie Brown that she won't pull the football from him if he just runs up and kicks it.

# Getting Ahead of It

You've already explained how the earth goes through cycles in climate. You've hopefully explained how science actually works: the process of never-ending trial and error, checking whether the same result will happen with each new similar iteration in the experiment.

You've also talked to them about the history of science: how the world accepted Aristotle's belief that objects of different weight fell at different rates. That was the "consensus" *for 2000 years*, but he was wildly wrong, and amazingly so easy to disprove. (Galileo disproved it easily in 1589 by dropping two balls of different weights from a balcony on the Leaning Tower of Pisa; you can do the same thing with your kids from some high structure with one light object and one heavy object).

There were many other such scientific "consensus" blunders: from people believing the earth was flat, the earth not being the center of the universe, no need to wash hands to avoid disease, to the more recent consensus that the universe was static (even Einstein believed in the long-held belief in the static nature of the universe, despite his own Theory of Relativity compelling the opposite conclusion).

Kids now can also see how the great scientists of the day got it wrong when it came to the Covid-19 shutdown of 2020-21. They were wrong about the effectiveness of shutting down everything (one critical study by a professor at Johns Hopkins University showed that even assuming the most generous allowances, the shutdown reduced overall deaths by at best one-fifth of one percent.[37]) Scientists told us the virus resulted from a dirty "wet" market in Wuhan, arising from someone who ate a live bat or "pangolin," which "jumped" to humans from there. Scientists declared anyone who thought it had escaped from that virus lab only a mile away was crazy, even if that lab was, well, *just a mile away and the only such lab in all of China*. And even if that lab was well known for its sloppy handling and manipulation of viruses.

Yes, the *lab* theory was the crazy one. Those same scientists agreed only two and a half years later that the virus almost certainly *did* come from a lab, but in all fairness they really, really thought no one would remember what they had said before.

People masked up, but we now know masks didn't stop any spread (Dr. Fauci was right the first time he insisted people *not* wear a mask, even though he later admitted his unstated actual intention was to prevent a run on masks because there weren't enough available at the time). The mortality rate was much lower than scientists initially claimed (by a factor of 85 times lower, per a study from Stanford University only one month after the panicked shutdown in March, 2020[38]).

The government denied the reality of natural immunity for those who were previously infected with Covid and also banned the use of therapeutics such as Ivermectin, which were quite effective for many users. By contrast, the vaccines were far less effective than the CDC had claimed. In fact, it became questionable whether they worked at all: It didn't appear to help prevent spreading or getting the disease. It may have even made immunity less effective, and triggered the heart condition myocarditis in many recipients. It may have led to many other problematic side effects.

Other than that, the vaccines were awesome.

The key here is to show one simple fact: *Scientists are not gods.* In fact, they get it wrong very often, at least the first time they present any "out-there" hypothesis.

And with this gloriously imperfect backdrop in science, you can proceed to laugh at the cartoonishly absurd arena of global warming.

## Laughing at It and Dismissing It

You can have a lot of fun with global warming.

First, there's always the fact it was called "Global Warming," but then the media and elites had to change it to "Climate Change." Why? The planet wasn't quite warming as the know-betters had predicted. On top of that, point out that it was originally Global *Cooling* in the seventies and early eighties.

It makes your head spin. This of course calls their "expertise" into question. Give your children examples of how confusing it would be if you were told it was Thursday, but no, it's actually Sunday. No, now it's actually Tuesday.

Now we're playing basketball. Suddenly the ball changes and the other team is playing football, then soccer, and then badminton. What a country!

You're a boy, then a girl, then a 25-year old rock star from the sixties, then a black professional NBA star. In fact, you're Kobe Bryant, brought back to life. Sure, people *think* that you're only 5' 9", but those are just haters.

You get the idea. But Global Warming provides so much more. It explains *everything* that's going wrong in your world or even in your own life. It's been blamed not only for hurricanes and droughts (no evidence to support it. In the U.S. at least, there's been *no* increase in droughts since the 1890s).

There's even more. Did you know that climate change increases animal bites, mental health issues and even acne? Well, it does. Climate change also caused at least one beer shortage, a building collapse in England, the creation of ISIS, rising insurance premiums, kidney stones, prostitution, teenage drinking and homelessness. And those massive waves of illegal immigrants surging at America's border? Yep, Climate Change is the culprit—not system-wide corruption, brutal cartel violence, and endless debilitating cyclical poverty of the countries from which they arrive, as you might have theorized.[39] *That* theory is *so* 2010s.

In fact, just Google any word that comes to mind and add "climate change" to it and you'll probably find some study suggesting a connection between the two.[40] It's a bonding game the whole family can play (and laugh about).

That girl didn't want to go out with you? Climate Change.

You arrived late to lacrosse practice? Climate Change.

You didn't turn in your homework? Climate Change.

Your high school basketball team lost the homecoming game? Climate Change.

You see, Climate Change isn't just an explanation for extreme weather anymore. It explains *everything*. Wars, hunger, disease, racism, and brain freeze. I'd compare it to it being both a floor wax *and* a dessert topping, from the old Saturday Night Live parody commercial, but Climate Change is actually far more versatile.

Dismissing Global Warming and Climate Change is actually easy when you realize that it dismisses itself. From the hypocrite leaders who fly around in private jets to electric vehicles whose manufacturing of them actually create *more* carbon emissions than fuel-powered cars, to wealthy elites who buy properties on the coast that they claim are about to get covered in water, you've got a treasure trove to work with.

But remember the process: Get ahead of it. Talk to your kids *before* they hear about it from anyone else.

Here's a sample conversation with your daughter Becky, 7 years old. You're driving to Costco.

*Dad: Hey, Becks... You want to hear something really funny?*
*Becky: Sure!*
*Dad: A bunch of silly people think that we can control the temperature of the earth!*
*Becky: What? That sounds silly. Wait... are they democrats?*
*Dad: You got it! They think that by people driving around in cars like this and even breathing and burping and making toots we're going to make the earth hot, hot, hot! And so they want us to stop doing all that stuff.*
*Becky: That's crazy. How can they think that?*
*Dad: Oh, you know the democrats. They're afraid of everything!* [Pointing] *"Look at that leaf, it's going to crash into our car! NOOO!"*
*Becky (Laughing): Why are they always afraid?*
*Dad: It's funny, because they forget that the air and water is cleaner now more than ever, people are living longer than ever—you*

*know, because of America and all the cool stuff it invented. But they want to go back to caveman days, I suppose. What do you think? You want to go back to caveman days?*

    *Becky: Heck, no!*

    *Dad: But you know what's funny even about that?*

    *Becky: What's that?*

    *Dad: If they did turn it all off, we'd have to go back to fire to cook everything and for warmth. Guess what would happen if they did that? They'd get even more bad stuff for the environment!*

    *Becky (laughing): Well that wouldn't make any sense.*

    *Dad: I think you're right!*

    *Becky: So what do they want us to do?*

    *Dad: Oh, they want us to stop using fuel and other energy like that. They want us to use wind power and power from the sun instead. Do you see any problems with that?*

    *Becky: What happens when there's no wind, or if it's nighttime?*

    *Dad (impressed): Good point! And there's an even bigger problem with those things: They don't really work because you can't store the energy in any serious way. Oops!*

    *Becky: So why do they want those things? It doesn't make any sense!*

    *Dad: Why do you think, Becks?*

    *Becky (thinking a bit): Maybe they want it for a different reason?*

    *Dad: You're definitely getting there, sweetie.*

    *Becky: Because it's a way of controlling people that way?*

And so on… There are so many conversations like this just in the global warming realm alone: the constant missed deadlines by which the ice caps were supposed to have melted, the changing theories of what will happen, the inability to gauge temperature in a consistently accurate way, the fact that climate always changes on its own, anyway. The absurdity of the idea that we can change the weather, climate, or natural disasters.

*Mom: I really don't want to go to work tomorrow. I think I'll just command the sun not to set.*
*Katie: You can't do that, Mom! That's silly!*
*Mom (Smiling): Sorry, I was just thinking like a democrat. It'll pass.*

Remember: Kids *love* talking about absurd things. And as far as absurdities go, global warming is among the greatest of all time.

## America the Less Than Beautiful

You're seeing it and hearing it: America is such a bad country that perhaps we shouldn't even evoke the word *America*, lest it might make someone feel threatened. In case you thought that's an exaggeration, that was an actual proposal: a Stanford University professor listed *America* as one of many words that students—and any decent person, really—should no longer say or write. It just might offend some people.

Who might those people be? He didn't bother to investigate. But trust him: even if it's just a handful of people, that's enough to justify everyone else changing their everyday language to avoid talk of That-Which-Should-Never-Be-Mentioned. *America* should be the new "N" word.

## Identifying the Issue

The woke mob is out to minimize America and its historical values, and only amplify the negative aspects of America's history. To hear it from the Left, you'd think the entire *modus operandi* of America was to bring in slaves and kill native populations or anyone who didn't look like a proper white land-owning European male Christian. They begrudgingly agreed to allow white European female Christians, too, but only because they were necessary to breed more white European Christians.

According to our woke betters, we purposely brought infected blankets to Native Americans to hasten the deaths of these innocent and peace-loving people. When smallpox and other diseases didn't do the job, white soldiers broke every single treaty and otherwise deceived, raped, tortured, and killed innocent native peoples. You know it's true because you saw *Dances with Wolves*, like, three times.

And can we talk about how they wouldn't even count a black as a full person? It's right there in the Constitution you conservatives quote all the time: those Founding Fathers agreed to only count blacks as *three-fifths of a person*.* How ... er ... dehumanizing!

America doesn't get a break: America oppressed women, who didn't get the vote until the 1920s. America oppressed Hispanics, Asians, and Jews. Well, people really don't talk much more about how America oppressed Asians and Jews because Asians and Jews are doing fine now. So perhaps Americans are just *selectively* oppressive about some minorities. They're discerning in their discrimination, if you will.

There were also mass slaughters of babies in the womb and a decades-long eugenics program. Well, eugenics and abortion were actually passion projects of the Left, so you may not hear much about those. But you get the idea.

Columbus was ever so bad. His entire agenda wasn't to discover new lands and opportunities for Europe. It was to kill and enslave native tribes. Oh, how much better the Americas would be had the Europeans never arrived.

America was *really* founded in 1619 to expand slavery, not your precious "1776." That's just an inconsequential moment in history no more than the passing of the baton from one evil

---

* It's true it's in the Constitution, but the suggestion is misleading and actually the very opposite of the intent the Left claims. The 3/5ths figure was a compromise between North and South during the creation of the Constitution. The North didn't want to count slaves in the national census at all because it would give more representational power to the South in Congress. And it was actually the Southern states which wanted them fully counted because they wanted that power. So the two sides struck a compromise: Slaves would be counted as 3/5th of a person for representational purposes.

enslaving empire (the British) to another (the Americans). So don't let conservatives fool you with this distracting deviation from *real* history.

Also, the Founding Fathers were secular, despite what you think and even if all fifty states have the word *God* or *Supreme Being* in their constitutions. They created America as a secular nation to shirk off the shackles of oppressive religion. In fact, they were agnostics and atheists who were skeptical of religion, if not downright hostile to it. So, the Constitution forbade the exhibition of religion anywhere, and certainly teaching it in public schools. To do so would probably be child abuse.

Naturally, due to the inherent systemic racism of America from its very founding, the last thing your child should do is stand for the National Anthem or American Flag, let alone recite some meaningless words pledging allegiance to it.

In fact, take a knee if you *do* hear the National Anthem, wherever you might be on campus at the time, lest someone mistake that you respect it. You wouldn't want that.

## Getting Ahead of It

On this subject, there is so much (trigger warning) ammunition. There are at least three ways: (1) America's history, including its record of constant social improvement to the point it is now the *least* racist country in the world; (2) America's inventions, discoveries, and cultural contributions to the world, and (3) The rest of the world's desire to move to America more than any other country in the world.

### American History

There's no better way to appreciate American history than to learn American history. Not only that, but it's also exciting: the American Revolution was the first revolution based on an *idea*. That idea was liberty, that man was in charge of his own destiny, and that dictatorships rob men of their dignity, self-expression, and civilization's very ability to progress.

George Washington's steadfast belief in a free America, independent of Britain, held the country together. You can smell the stench of the men, the horses, and the burnt gunpowder as he struggles his way through the six years of war, constantly cheating death and defying the persistent predictions of the collapse of his army and the American cause. His stepping down from the presidency to allow the peaceful changing of the presidency was also a first in history.

The country was tested again and again in the War of 1812, the Civil War, and the Spanish War. Each time, America came out on top, spreading liberty to more and more countries. Then came World War I and World War II, in which America not only saved Europe from collapse both times, but became a world superpower, spreading liberty throughout even more regions of the world.

All the while, America broke the shackles of millennia of wrongs, particularly of slavery, then of segregation. It brought justice for those wrongly imprisoned in the Japanese internment camps. It rectified much of its wrongs against Native Americans, creating better opportunities for them economically, educationally, and socially. It opened opportunities for women, minorities, and religions of every kind.

No other country sought to redress wrongs it had itself made, as America did. America was and remains a country constantly in a state of self-evaluation and self-improvement, always seeking ways "to form a more perfect union."

Did France ever do that? Germany? The Czech Republic? Brazil? Name one country in which this self-improvement mechanism is not only in the DNA of its people, but in its *founding* documents, the most powerful one being the right to petition the government for grievances and peacefully assemble in the First Amendment.*

---

* Only in relatively recent modern times have other countries finally adopted codification of similar rights in respective their charters or constitutions. See, generally, https://en.wikipedia.org/wiki/Freedom_of_assembly. It is a testament, once again, to the extraordinary influence of American ideas.

So our Constitution itself actually enabled people to stand up for their rights—and secure them. In the 1920s, women fought for and secured their right to vote. In the 1950s, Rosa Parks, an ordinary black woman of the American South, refused to give up her seat on the bus. She became a hero, securing a landmark place in history after the country, applying America's founding principles, ultimately sided with her. It was her action which in turn enabled another rising voice of freedom, Martin Luther King, Jr. to harken to the words of the Declaration of Independence and the United States Constitution themselves that all men were created equal, that all people are free.

The stories don't stop there: from Asians to Jews to Hispanics to gays and even transgenders, the stories of ever-increasing freedoms and rights continued—sometimes going too far (the "right" to a basic income, the "right" to healthcare).

No other country ever adopted such an extraordinary self-correcting system. While other countries certainly have judicial systems and effectuate change from time to time, they tend to change begrudgingly, resistant to change. America's very structure seems designed around self-improvement not only of itself, but to encourage the self-actualization of all its individual citizens.

American history is the story of leadership not only in the spread of liberty, but ever-increasing rights. The rest of the world only follows.

Tell this to your children, and they'll not only walk with fierce pride in their country, but they'll proselytize America's cause for the rest of their lives.

## America's Inventions

Not yet convinced of America's awesomeness? *Well wait, there's more!* One of the staggering insights you should talk about with your kids is how the vast majority of all modern inventions, discoveries, and cultural offerings we enjoy today come from one particular country—the United States of America.

Yes, from the time of the Civil War on, America created virtually every modern convenience we use today. I call if the "look around you" test, as in "look around you, and see how almost every invention since the 1860s was invented here in America."

It's not that hard: there's the suspension bridge, the telegraph, the telephone, the airplane, the car, the skyscraper, air conditioning, the typewriter, cameras and photography (as we think of it), the copy machine, Morse code, movies, television, radar, the washing machine and dryer, blue jeans, the refrigerator, the harnessing of electricity, the light bulb, the assembly line, hearing aids, the magnetic stripe card and credit cards, computers, the mobile phone, email, the Internet, the smart phone, search engines, translation apps, dictation apps, artificial intelligence apps, and virtually all other critical everyday apps and software (graphics, word processing, spreadsheets, etc.), video games, GPS, and Lasik.

Then there are the less celebrated but powerful inventions we rarely think of but couldn't live without: Post-it notes, the ball-point pen, the razor and the electric razor, the hand-held blow dryer, and, perhaps most important: wheels on luggage.*

Also, lest you think there was some unique creative gene in the DNA of Americans, it was first-generation immigrants from eastern European countries who invented many of these inventions. Yes, you might point out individuals from many other countries came up with the prototypes or concepts for many of America's inventions. For example, the wheels on luggage concept first was invented by a Yugoslavian, Alfred Krupa. He attempted to patent this invention (among others) by contacting authorities in Belgrade, Yugoslavia and even the British Embassy, but they weren't interested. He eventually gave up on the idea.

---

\* There are also all the smaller items in-between: the stop sign, tabulation machines, smoke detectors, bottle caps, zippers, mousetraps, Kevlar, frozen food, the disposable diaper, chocolate chip cookies, the electric traffic light, pantyhose, and fly swatters.

Also, a Frenchman first came up with the concept of photography, and an Englishman came up with the concept of movies. But without the free markets of America, which rewarded and protected ideas and which streamlined the process for capitalizing on ideas with patents, such ideas never took off in those other countries. Only America's unique form of property-protecting capitalism allowed such great ideas to come to meaningful and universal fruition.

### So Much for the Population Bomb Scare

Notably, despite horrific predictions of mass world-wide hunger by the year 1990 (thanks to the hysteria Paul Ehrlich pushed on the world in his best-selling but debunked *The Population Bomb* [1968]), we now have more food than ever. That's thanks in particular to American innovations in animal and crop genetics, advanced machinery and robotics, chemicals, and farm organization. In fact, as a result of such American innovations, total farm production nearly *tripled* between 1948 and 2017, even as land and labor used in farming declined.[41] In this arena, the rest of the world benefitted yet again from America's ingenuity. Hunger and poverty not only did not increase; it declined dramatically (see discussion on capitalism, below).

### Indoor Plumbing, How We Love Thee

One of the most significant yet underappreciated and unsung American inventions has been indoor plumbing. Considering its reliability and ubiquity, the world now takes it for granted—until disaster strikes. Ask the victims of the great New Zealand earthquake in Christchurch of February 2011. The 6.3 magnitude earthquake, which followed a 7.1 magnitude earthquake just half a year earlier, destroyed the town's water and sewage systems. City officials there instructed their residents not to drink, shower or use the toilets due to the lack and quality of a water supply. Many had to resort to digging a hole in the backyard to deposit sewage.[42]

I'd guess those residents probably lost any romance they might have once held for the bucolic and simpler days of yore. I'd also guess these residents got a quick appreciation on the meaning of *infrastructure*.

Similar disasters happen all over the world, also leaving innocent residents stranded from their assumed conveniences of everyday life. As the Joni Mitchell song famously quipped: "Don't it always seem to go / That you don't know what you've got till it's gone" ("Big Yellow Taxi," 1970). The modern internal plumbing which we take for granted today, with its standards of appropriate pressure and gauges to maximize appropriate ingress, egress, and flow, all conveniently coursing through pipes hidden behind walls and under floors, was all invented in America. That includes not just the indoor piping, but modern kitchens, toilets, bathtubs, and showers in even the poorest neighborhoods. Such plumbing and its related appliances allow people to cook and clean, bathe, and maintain hygiene with extraordinary regularity and convenience at little cost, to say nothing of avoiding a myriad of diseases.[43]

The list of American-made inventions is actually so long that it would take the entirety of the pages of this book without tabs or paragraphs breaks, to list even half of them. Recall the game my family sometimes plays at dinner: Name an invention made in America and keep going around the table until someone stumbles and can't think of one after five seconds. Then he or she is out, and the game continues with the remaining players until the last one standing. (There can be challenges about whether the invention, discovery or contribution actually came from America, I suppose, but that's what internet search engines are for.) It's lots of fun, and it greatly helps in the education of your children.

Then we play the same game, except this time inventions coming out of Cuba, Vietnam, North Korea, Venezuela, China, and the former Soviet Union. That game doesn't last as long: It turns out there is less innovation than you might have expected from those Socialist paradises. The good news is you'll discover the crickets in your house very fast.

In fact, the only other country that seems to produce similar prolific output in inventions is Israel. That tiny country has produced among the highest number of inventions since its founding in 1948, and has more companies listed on the NASDAQ than all of Europe combined. It's also first in the world for total expenditures on research and development (as a percentage of GDP), and first in the world in scientific publications.[44] There are now more than thirty technology companies in Israel which are each valued over $1 billion, again more than all of Europe combined.[45]

And the reason for that is the subject of our next area of glory: capitalism.

*Capitalism*

Capitalism goes hand in hand with the American story. For those who dismiss capitalism as inherently evil, bringing out the worst in human beings and focused only the selfish needs of the individual, one need only know that poverty and hunger have plummeted since America's industrial entrepreneurship took off after the Civil War. Before that time, virtually all but a select elite few in the world lived in extreme poverty, substantially more than 90%.[46] By 2015, that rate was down to 10%—and still falling.[47]

Not only this, the number of people living in extreme poverty worldwide declined *by 80 percent* in just the short time period between 1970 and 2006.[48] It is a truly remarkable achievement, but it doesn't receive a lot of media coverage. In fact, chances are you've never learned this in high school, college, or graduate school. Why? Perhaps because it highlights the success of capitalism.

But there is no escaping it: as American Enterprise Institute (AEI) president Arthur Brooks said: "[I]t was the free enterprise system, American style, which is our gift to the world." No other socioeconomic system has done more to eradicate poverty. Ever.[49]

The Foundation for Economic Education's (FEE) Steven Horwitz, noted the world is *120 times better off today* than in 1800 as a result of capitalism, in terms of gains in average human consumption and life expectancy (that's increased life expectancy by *decades*, not just by a few years). Competition has also made education, art, and culture available to almost everyone. Even the poorest now "have access through the Internet and TV to concerts, books, and works of art that were exclusively the province of the wealthy for centuries."[50] According to World Health Organization (WHO) data, because of better access to medicine and better living standards, mortality rates for children under the age of five declined by 49 percent in just the short period from 1990 to 2013.[51]

You need not look far to see it yourself: Perhaps you have a gardener working for you. A sanitation man picks up your garbage once a week. A woman comes once a week to clean your house or look after your kids. A plumber comes to fix your sink. Each of them has more than any king or rich man had only a hundred years ago. They each can travel further than any such king ever hoped, and quicker, at a reasonable price. They usually have a car, a cell phone, entertainment (TV, movies, radio and music), air-conditioning, refrigerators, access to plenty of food—and a good variety of it. Their kids go to school. They have access to medical care.

Clothing is abundant and super cheap: Most kids have multiple times the number of shirts, pants, underwear and socks as did any royalty of the old days. Virtually no one wears threadbare or ragged clothing anymore—not even the most destitute.

Anyone can exchange messages, real time video calls and make public announcements with friends and loved ones and the public at large across the world in an instant—for free. We can even cheaply shave, get "mani-pedis," haircuts, blow-dries and hair coloring. All of these used to be lavishly expensive luxuries reserved for the royalty wearing purple coats and sitting in the back of horse carriages, who occasionally noticed the multitude of beggars on the filthy street staring back at them as they passed them by.

Not surprisingly, the biggest recent gains against poverty and mortality have occurred in countries which decided to open up their markets, such as China, Vietnam, and India.[52] And where did they get the idea of opening their markets? You can hear the answer loudly and proudly in the chants at American sporting events and rallies all over the nation: *USA! USA!*

In fact, in the United States, some of our greatest advances in lifting every American out of poverty were already happening as early as the fifties and sixties. Poverty in the U.S. was plummeting—until President Lyndon Johnson declared war on it. With his combination of welfare handouts, wealth redistributions and tax increases, it only disincentivized work and increased dependence. It proved the timeless truism: government intervention almost always hurts those it is intended to help.[53] Yes, that's irony for you.

To see the converse of what a world would look like without capitalism, we need only look at countries who have made the Noble Switch to socialism:

Cuba went from a promising island economy to a country where citizens have to make the most from scraps they once had before their socialist revolution. Because Cuba is an island, it was almost a perfect laboratory to prove the point: the tools, appliances and even the cars are noticeably all from the fifties. In this way, Cuba looks like it's frozen in time in that bygone era. The only thing that seemed to change over the decades were Fidel Castro's wrinkles and the color of his beard.

Venezuela likewise chose to make the Great Leap Forward in the late 1990s. Like Cuba before its socialism, Venezuela was also one of the most economically vibrant countries south of the United States. It was spectacularly rich in oil reserves. But the country decided socialism was worth a shot, and almost immediately the country spiraled into misery. As with most socialist countries, its two back-to-back dictators (Hugo Chavez and Nicholas Maduro) started disappearing enemies and silencing dissent.

To go there now, you'd see people clawing over one another for bread, literally chasing small pieces of it that some autocrat from the government throws at them. Look at the videos; they follow the same swarming pattern pigeons make when they likewise scurry for bread. It's also common to sell rotten meat, because, well ... what else is there?[54] People routinely eat from garbage dumps, bodies pile up at morgues and are never processed. Tragically and almost unbelievably, mothers tell their children that they will have to give them away, because they can no longer take care of them.[55]

There are many such countries, and every one that switched from capitalism, or any form of free markets, invariably deliver far worse results for their people. By contrast, countries that had once been socialist and switched to capitalism tended to thrive. How much thriving occurred depended on how swiftly a country adopted capitalism and abandoned socialism. For example, Ukraine and Russia, which adopted economic freedoms slowly, ended up far behind another country that had also formerly belonged to the Soviet Bloc, the Czech Republic. That country went far beyond the others in GDP per person, income equality, rule of law, political freedom, and life expectancy.[56]

Sweden and other Nordic countries learned this lesson, and thankfully reversed course. Sweden in particular had done so well economically before the 1970s that it decided to turn itself into a generous welfare state, because they figured they just had so much wealth to share. It embraced socialism between around 1970 and 1990. This plummeted the country into horrific economic malaise. Since 1990, however, both conservative and social democratic-led governments moved back to the political center and brought back free-market principals. The country roared back economically, socially, and otherwise.[57]

Despite capitalist critics who fondly cite to these countries as great examples of "socialism that works," no one should view Denmark, Norway, and Sweden as "socialist," let alone socialist utopias. Far from it: they *strongly* embrace free-market principles, including property rights. They now have stricter immigration policies, tightened eligibility requirements for welfare benefit systems, are far tougher on crime, and have adopted far more business-friendly policies than ever.[58]

Likewise, Israel's founders envisioned a socialist country, and after three decades realized that inflation and other socialist policies were crippling the nation. By the 1980s, Israel effectively dropped its socialism. It did so by dramatically reducing its government spending, embracing a "start-up" culture of innovation, and opening up markets to the private sector and protecting property rights. It now produces more GDP per capita than most other countries.[59]

Even former communist bastions China and Vietnam have embraced significant free-market principles, allowing them each to grow into economic powerhouses, certainly relative to their prior "pure" socialism. Only Cuba and North Korea are the remaining wallflowers at the Great Global Capitalism prom.

The bottom line: you can love everything you want about socialism, except socialism itself.

### America's Medical and Scientific Discoveries

The marvels of America don't stop with all the cool stuff it invented which people use every day and which have become absolute necessities (refrigeration, washer/dryer, telephone, car, internet). Our medical and scientific discoveries have also shaped the world as we know it. Here are just some of the health and medical advances:

From anesthesia to the discovery of how insects transfer diseases, the electrocardiograph, the first heart valve surgery, the Human Genome Project and the discovery and decoding of DNA, the discovery of life's mystery messenger RNA (specifically how genetic instructions are carried to the cell's protein manufacturing center, where all of life's processes begin), medical diagnostics and treatment (nuclear medicine,

producing radioisotopes to diagnose and treat disease, design-
ing imaging technology), the polio vaccine (among many other
vaccines and cures), the creation of blood banks, emergency
health plans, lung and bone marrow transplants, the discovery
of "good" and "bad" cholesterol, the Heimlich maneuver, the
breathalyzer, and prenatal DNA screening, there is no country
that has impacted the world's health more profoundly than the
United States.

Then there are America's incredible other scientific inventions and discoveries: Harnessing the power of the atom
(nuclear power and reactors), bringing safe water to millions
(removing arsenic from drinking water, making contaminated
water safe to drink, ultraviolet light to kill water-borne bacteria
that cause dysentery); lighter-weight metals and alloys that save
fuel and maintenance costs and enable cleaner, more efficient
engines; confirmation of the "Big Bang" theory of the origin of
the universe; the mapping of the universe and the dark side of
the moon; x-rays; discovery of the secrets of matter (identification of six kinds of quarks, three types of neutrinos and the
Higgs particle, changing our view of how the material world
works); the discovery of Dark Energy; the discovery of 22 more
elements of the periodic table; a "magic sponge" to clean up oil
spills; high-tech coatings to reduce friction; levitated trains with
magnets; synthetic rubber; nylon and Teflon; the discovery that
it was an asteroid collision which killed the dinosaurs; the discovery of radon gas and its dangers; simulated reality software
for trains, planes, automobiles and thousands of other objects;
the neutrino; gamma ray bursts; artificial photosynthesis; and
advanced fusion technology.[60]

Oh, and we put a man on the moon.

### America's Cultural Contributions

Of course, there are things beyond the practical and con-
venient; beyond just making life more manageable or efficient.
America and capitalism have influenced the world far beyond
just its inventions and discoveries. It gave us things that make

life worth living, enrich it, and help people self-actualize. Even that concept, *self-actualization*, developed and described by American psychiatrist Abraham Maslow as "the desire to become more and more what one is, to become everything that one is capable of becoming," would be unimaginable in a world where one thinks predominantly of just subsisting.

### Freedom as a Gift Itself

It began not just by the concept of the right to profit and keep one's wages, or to capitalize from new ideas. America also gave us the concept of a Constitutional Republic, with the centrality of the individual, liberty, and freedom of speech as the founding principles of our nation. It gave the world the concepts of government accountability and checks and balances. No other nation at the time of America's founding offered anything close. The world noted America's success, and other countries developed similar modes of liberty and accountability. As we noted above, almost 90 nations are now considered "free" or "mostly free."

### Oh, No, It's NOT Only Rock n' Roll

Freedom alone would be enough. But think of all the other cultural gifts from America: in music, America created Ragtime, the Blues, Big Band "Swing," Rock n' Roll, American Folk music, Country and Western, Jazz, Rap and Hip-Hop. That's not to say that other countries didn't or don't have their own local music flavors; far from it. But like so many other things from America, American music and styles seem to project outward, take root and grow everywhere they land. For example, while modern pop music in Korea (K-Pop) has its own flair and Korean stars, it derives entirely from American pop. Go anywhere else in the world and you'll hear popular music on the radio just like American music. It'll almost always be in the national language, but the style is decidedly American.

But wait, you say: What about the British Invasion of the sixties, seventies, and beyond? Didn't they give us the Beatles, the Rolling Stones, Pink Floyd, the Who, Elton John, Radiohead, Queen, U2, and much more? What about Abba from Sweden and AC/DC from Australia?

It's true they weren't from America, but listen to the music: *All* their sounds and styles *come from* American rock n' roll, folk, or rap/hip-hop music. *All* of it.

And that's to say nothing of the electric guitars and other instruments on which they play, and much of the recording technology and acoustic development through which musicians distribute and broadcast their music, and the technology through which people hear their music (the LP, the compact disc, and now downloading of music from the internet, all of which were also American inventions).

*Movies and TV*

Like several other inventions, the creation of the motion picture may not have technically originated in the U.S., but it was the U.S. that fully realized and executed its massive potential. The word "Hollywood" alone conjures up visions of movie stars and Oscar nights and Western gunslingers getting ready for the shootout. From the very early movies in the early 20th Century to *Star Wars, Back to the Future, Terminator, Rambo, Rocky, Pirates of the Caribbean, Avatar, Die Hard, Top Gun, Mission Impossible,* and all those superhero movies (to say nothing of all the massively successful kids' movies from Disney, Pixar and Dreamworks), Europe and the rest of the world eat up American entertainment. In 2006, *64 percent of all movies* shown in the European Union were American. By comparison, only 3 percent of the movies shown in the USA were from Europe.*

So great is American influence that many people who have never been to America actually feel they have a good idea of

---

* American influence is so great that former President Jacques Chirac of France sought to limit the number of American films that French cinemas could show, because he did not want to see "European culture sterilized or obliterated by American culture for economic reasons that have nothing to do with real culture." But that's France for you. The French culture *gendarmes* also wanted to prohibit the word "e-mail" (they prefer *poste électronique*) and the word "weekend" (*fin de la semaine*).

what living in America is like. Stereotypes that come from American film and TV even form international opinion. For example, people regularly refer to cowboys, oil tycoons, and the action heroes in the *Rambo* and *Die Hard* series when referring to American foreign policy. Likewise, people may feel that they know New York City after seeing enough episodes of *Friends* or *Seinfeld*.[61]

The United States not only invented movies, but gave us theaters and the affordability to watch their favorites stars and stories. From Greta Garbo and Clark Gable to Dwayne Johnson and Jennifer Aniston, from movies like *Gone with the Wind* to all the Disney and Pixar movies, the *Star Wars* and *Rocky* and *Terminator* franchises, the rest of the world embraces our particular brand of storytelling. They may find them unsophisticated and lacking in art, just like our fast food and crazy coffee bastardizations, but damn if they don't consume them like termites to wood.

American cinema has also inspired cinema elsewhere. India has been pouring out legions of movies to its massive audience (so-called "Bollywood"), as well as China, South Korea, and England. Now, with the advent of cheaper technology, we see the production of far more foreign films than ever, seemingly from all of the world.

Likewise, TV (remember: another American invention) allowed networks to create a bevy of new program types of entertainment including game shows, news programs, soap operas, mystery shows, westerns and, of course, situation comedies (sit-coms). International TV stations not only air American shows (*The Simpsons, Friends, Cheers, Modern Family*), but also mimic their talk shows, game shows and talent shows. Even the news programs copy the same format as American news.

Cable TV (there's yet another American invention. *Yawn*) expanded the variety, quantity, and quality of American shows, creating such international phenoms as *The Sopranos, Dallas, Sex and the City, ER,* and more recently *Breaking Bad* and *Yellowstone*. It also spawned the first international news 24-hour network,

CNN, which in turn led to the BBC, Fox News, MSNBC, and so many other cable news channels both in America and abroad.

The Apple Mac and its progeny and all other personal computers, iPods and MP3 players, smartphones, tablets, and the internet (again, all American inventions) allowed even greater access to such entertainment. It also contributed to culture and commerce, and to the world of information writ large. They connected us like never before in history, and the exchange of culture exploded like never before, too.

Thanks to all such things, opportunities and employment also expanded for everyone around the world. Anyone could stay in and work from their home countries yet work for jobs in the US, many of which didn't even exist in their own country, or which offered much higher salaries.

A pretty good gig, no?

*Art and Architecture*

America has contributed to the arts as well, both in painting and sculpture, distinct from that of Europe. American artists rooted themselves in the everyday, and the scenes include majestic landscapes, still life, scenes of home and farm and hearth, and of course the chronicle of our history.[62] The Hudson River School focused on realism of the western landscape—a new art frontier in its own rite—as America expanded to the West.

Since 1900 American art revolted against tradition. "To hell with the artistic values," artist Robert Henri announced. He was the leader of what critics called the Ashcan school of painting, after the group›s portrayals of the squalid aspects of city life. American realism became a new direction for American visual artists. The Ashcan painter George Bellows and others developed socially conscious imagery in their works.

The photographer Alfred Stieglitz led the Photo-Secession movement, which created pathways for photography as an emerging art form. Soon the Ashcan school artists gave way to American modernism.

After World War I many American artists rejected the modern trends, instead depicting American urban and rural scenes. The city scenes of Edward Hopper, the rural imagery of Andrew Wyeth, and the Americana of everyday life of Norman Rockwell pushed unique scenes of realism. Likewise, "Precisionist Art" highlighted sharply defined renderings of machines and architectural forms.

America then gave us the American Southwest art, Harlem Renaissance, "New Deal" art, Abstract Expressionism, Lyrical Abstraction, Conceptual Art, Postminimalism, Earth Art, Video, Performance art, Installation art, Abstract Expressionism, Color Field Painting, Hard-edge painting, Minimal Art, Op art, Pop Art, Photorealism and New Realism. All these extended the boundaries of Contemporary Art in the mid-1960s through the 1970s.

Members of the next artistic generation mixed media, another level of abstraction. Among them were Robert Rauschenberg and Jasper Johns, who used photos, newsprint, and discarded objects in their art. Pop artists such as Andy Warhol and Roy Lichtenstein made "art" out of everyday objects and images of American popular culture—Coca-Cola bottles, soup cans, and even comic strips.[63]

All such art had its powerful effect on the rest of the world—a new freedom in artistic expression. Many of us may lament its impact on our culture, as we might lament fast-food or rap music's impact, but no one can deny its influence upon the world. America met a world demand for new avenues of expression.

In architecture, America was even more impactful. In the 1800s, the United States built its government, and "Revival architecture" became popular. Thomas Jefferson, himself an architect, sought to imitate Greek architecture which would well reflect the ideals of the early American government. This spawned many other movements (neoclassical, Gothic revival, Beaux Arts/Renaissance, Richardsonian Romanesque, and Chateau Architecture).

Most importantly, however, were the new architectural designs of the 1900s. Starting then, America contributed in the form of skyscrapers and the Prairie School (Frank Lloyd Wright). Coming first out of the Chicago School and New York, skyscrapers defined urban centers in large cities. Before America, the most floors any building could take was nine, which number was always unstable. (That, in addition to the problem that the indoor plumbing of the day could only accommodate so many floors.)

Today, every major metropolis dons some sort of skyscraper landscape—all thanks to another American innovation, the efficient and mass production of steel, without which there could be no tall buildings at all.

*Literature*

Europe and the rest of the world gobble up American authors as much as anything else American. They read books from Stephen King, Anne Tyler, Michael Crichton, Dan Patterson, Ken Follett, Jacqueline Susann, John Grisham, and Dan Brown, whether in English or translated. Like all other forms of entertainment, they're now easier than ever to access through online retailers, by download or in audible versions (both of which platforms, come to think of it, were invented in America. But I repeat myself.)

American authors first impacted the international scene after World War I, including Ernest Hemingway, T. S. Eliot, Robert Frost and John Steinbeck, and later Kurt Vonnegut, Truman Capote, JD Salinger, Joseph Heller and Norman Mailer. The number of American authors reaching the rest of the world accelerated with each decade.

Why? Perhaps because many of the books focused on the individual, on misfits and social outcasts clashing with society, or who viewed American society with disapproval or distrust.[64] As in one of the great American literature firsts, *The Adventures of Huckleberry Finn* by Mark Twain, American authors often used fiction to mock society—something they could only do thanks to America's primary value of freedom of speech. The rest of the world saw this as refreshing in its honesty, even liberating. Maybe it spoke to the concerns and feelings of citizens all over the world who didn't necessarily have the same freedoms to express themselves.[65] No matter what the reason, the world has absorbed American literature into its cultural DNA.

### *"Have it Your Way": Fast Food and Gourmet Coffee*

We're the country that developed fast food, and much of the equipment that could make food "fast"—the toaster, grinders, air fryers, microwaves, the refrigerator. We brought "Le Big Mac" to France and to the rest of the world. Likewise, KFC, Burger King, and the whole fast food and "take-away" food concept, with many countries developing their own versions of fast food (they're never as good, but that's not important right now). We've changed Chinese, Italian, Japanese, and Thai food among so many other national cuisines to make them more appealing and accessible to everyone.

My favorite twist on food is what California Pizza Kitchen did to pizza (my favorite is their Thai Chicken Pizza: No one had thought of that combination of flavors and food styles. Somehow, it's perfect). Then there's Americanized-style gourmet coffee from Starbucks, Coffee Bean, Pete's, and numerous others. Suddenly the world rejected the monolithic there-is-only-one-way-to-make-cappuccino from the coffee elitists of France or Italy. You could sweeten it up, mix it with whipped cream, cookies and cream and pumpkin syrup, make it a "half-caff" or otherwise "have it your way." Awesome.

You don't like that? Fine. But look at the line out that coffee shop door.

The rest of the world thinks it's awesome, too. If they didn't, you wouldn't see these coffee chains in virtually every country, just as we do in America.

And for those countries which don't yet have their Starbucks? Believe me, they can't wait. There's some reason for the lack of presence, for sure, but it ain't because they have different taste buds.

*The Supermarket*

More than a hundred years ago, Clarence Saunders opened the first "Piggly Wiggly" in Memphis, Tenn. He imagined a "self-service" model of shopping that drastically altered food shopping. In the days before, customers would pass a grocery list to a store clerk, who would then put items together for shoppers in one bag.

Saunders got it in his head to redesign food shopping, methodically arranging things in order to appeal to how customers shopped—for example, putting candy and other impulse items at the checkout. Piggly Wiggly also introduced shopping baskets, price-marked items, employees in uniform and the whole supermarket franchise model.

In short, shoppers now could browse and choose their own food. The products had to appeal and tempt the consumer. This led to a complete turnabout in marketing: Companies had to catch consumers' attention. Designers would strategically place their products on shelves. Stores would place candies and other kids' favorites at kids' eye levels, making it easy for them to woo their parents into various purchases. (So much for saving money…).

This began a true exploitation of America's other intellectual gift: branding intellectual property through trademarks after the U.S. Congress passed its first Trademark Act in 1881. This gave companies a way to officially assert rights in their products as their own and combat copycats and rivals. But until Piggly Wiggly, every store just had a specialty, like butchers, bakers, and florists. There was little use of trademarks.

Suddenly, these grocery stores could amalgamate costs, bringing down overhead. All of this brought prices down on every product with greater choice and quality, and created jobs. Branding through trademarks (the famous ones of Coca-Cola and McDonald's are easy examples) became commonplace and a powerful competitive business tool, largely due to Piggly Wiggly.

The America supermarket phenomenon became such a marvel that in 1957, Queen Elizabeth and Prince Philip joined President Eisenhower in a visit to a Maryland grocery store to see what the fuss was all about. The Queen was reportedly "bemused" by the grocery cart's little collapsible seat. She particularly liked how it made it easy to bring children.[66]

### Fashion and Clothing

The American fashion world has also delivered exceptional products to a ravenous world market: Coach, Calvin Klein, Ralph Lauren, Donna Karan, Tommy Hilfiger, Vera Wang, GUESS, Kenneth Cole, and of course Levi's Jeans. Perfumes and make-up brands include Estee Lauder, Michael Kors, and Calvin Klein's Obsession. We also produce affordable soaps, deodorants, feminine products, and razors, all of which impact daily lifestyles in all parts of the world. And virtually none of it would be available but for the greater free time and concept of disposable income (see below) America gave the world.

In clothing, blue jeans are everywhere in the world, as are shorts, t-shirts, baseball caps and visors, sneakers, and modern sunglasses.

And never forget the shoes. Men may need only a few pairs, but if she wants, any woman can now have more shoes than a leftist has complaints.

### The Creation of Leisure and "I Can Be Me"

In recreation, America invented virtually every video game on every smartphone, every virtual reality experience, and before that every pinball and arcade game. There's the recreational vehicle (RV), or mobile home, modern sunscreen, mountain biking and all the advances associated with it (dual suspension, 1 X 11 gears, dropper posts, titanium framing, tubeless tires). In fact, leisure in general exists predominantly as an American gift to the world: the very concept of a 48-hour, two-day weekend came from American Henry Ford.*

But the dye was already cast before Ford. America's inventions of efficiency and convenience (the cotton gin, the washing machine and dryer, refrigeration, air conditioning, and so on) were already minimizing laborious processes. Likewise, greater agricultural advances, automation and assembly-line production allowed for greater production, and less need for worker hours. The numbers reflect it: while most men worked more than 70 hours a week in the early 1800s, that number went down to 60 hours per week by end of that century. That number is now below 40 hours a week. This represents a swing from only 1.8 hours of free time per day in the early 1800s to more than 5.8 hours per day today.[67]

By the early twentieth century, the old Victorian ideals of decorum and self-restraint gave way to enjoying life, a new concept which society now considered good for one's overall well-being. Media and business promoted the concept of "having fun" to encourage all Americans to engage in leisure activities. It was America's inventions and discoveries that drove this new freedom. The culture relented in its rigidity because people now had much more time in the week to enjoy leisure, and demanded it.

This new sense of leisure soon traveled across the oceans to Europe. Business stepped up to offer goodies to meet the new demands: beach attire and accompanying beach stuff, new leisure clothing, new sporting equipment, hobbies, and far more entertainment than ever.

America soon became associated with endless possibilities and opportunities. You were suddenly much more than

---

* Don't think Ford acted out of benevolence. He proposed the 40-hour work week solely as a means to stem absenteeism and increase motivation among his workers. He saw his plan work immediately. In fact, not only did he stop losing money, his workers were so much better off and gained so much more money that they began to buy Ford's cars for themselves. See "Hankering for History, the History of the Weekend," https://hankeringforhistory.com/history-weekend/, 2014. This was another win for Ford, and another win for the positive effects of the market economy.

your work. America not only became the land where one could achieve great things, but supplied the concept of "achievement" to the rest of the world. With more leisure time for themselves, everyone could look forward not just to resting up, but to exploring—whatever "exploring" might mean to them. No one was now locked into his job. During one's free time, he could look for another job or even create a new business or even industry.

Think of Steven Jobs: If he had to work as a typical male in the early 1800s, he would have likely had no time even to *think* of creating an entirely new industry of personal computers (and digital music through the iPod, smartphones, tablets, Pixar and the dedicated Apple store business model), much less execute his ideas.

In short, instead of getting by, people could *aspire*. Dreams were something they could now actually pursue.

Come to think of it, this may have been America's greatest export of all.

### The World Wants to Come to America More than to Any Other Country

It won't shock anyone to learn that more people want to move to the United States than to any other country. According to the United Nations Department of Economic and Social Affairs, the United States far and away leads the world in total immigrant population: More than 46 million total immigrants are in the U.S., or roughly 15 percent of its population. The country with the second-largest immigrant population is Germany with just over 7 million immigrants. The next three are Russia, Saudi Arabia, and the United Kingdom.[68]

A Gallup poll found that 150 million adults say they would like to move to the U.S., giving it the undisputed title as the world's most desired destination for potential migrants since Gallup started tracking these patterns in 2007. Moreover, people who seek immigration to the United States come from virtually every corner of the world. And they're apparently not coming because of our vaunted "systemic" racism, either: Most of them come from Africa, China, and India.[69]

But that won't stop the left from talking about America like it's the worst country in the world. You can't help but feel like they're talking out of both sides of their mouths:

*Protester number 1: We are the freest nation in the world. We offer the most opportunities anyone could dream of. We should be a beacon for all those who suffer in other parts of the world! Open our borders and let them in!*

*Protester number 2: Yes! Also, we're the worst country in the world!*

Even in their hatred of America, the left just can't seem to pick a lane.

So getting ahead of it is easy. After talking about how great America is and its many inventions and contributions, as well as how it advanced civil rights and improved the lives of everyone, let your kids know their school and social media will say that America is racist, that capitalism is awful, and that we should be more like other countries—especially the nice socialist ones. But remember: Make sure to do it before the school or anyone else gets to them first. Sadly, these days this means you should probably start around the second year of nursery school.

## Laughing at It and Dismissing It

There are so many different approaches with which to talk to your children about America. One need only rattle off the uniqueness of its founding ideas, its spread of liberty and protection of other countries in both World Wars and beyond, its economic system and its resulting massive number of inventions and discoveries, and its cultural contributions.

Do it at the breakfast table, during short and long drives, waiting in line at the waterslide park, while you're doing grocery shopping. Anywhere and anytime. See a plane in the sky?

That was from America. The car we're driving and the modern road we're driving on? America. That guy wearing his cheap t-shirt and sunglasses, while simultaneously listening to music and riding his skateboard on the wrong side of the road without a helmet, smoking a cigarette from one hand and holding an e-cigarette on the other? America. *Wait, get off the road you idiot!*

Hey, Kenny, look at that crowd over there, protesting capitalism. They're filming it all with their smartphones. They're using their bullhorns and speakers to project their voices. They traveled to get here in their cars. Almost all of their protest signs are custom-ordered and prefabricated. Where did all those things and services come from? Capitalism.

*Irony*. It's a word your kid should get familiar with.

I understand talking to kids about all of America's contributions might be overwhelming and daunting. After all, the list is just far too long. No other country in the world has done so much good, and contributed as much, for the rest of the world. Not even close. So, mustering all America's successes feels like when your kid wins all the academic and athletic trophies at school. There's just not enough room in the car to take them all home. (Would that we parents all have that problem).

But that's the good news: there's so much on the list you can keep talking about it without ever repeating yourself. It's almost as long as the list of the left's failures and how often they've been wrong.

Consider playing the "It came from America" game I mentioned before. There's also the "Kings and Queens" game: ask your kids how much better off they are than kings and queens from just a hundred years ago. From this they'll also learn the words *appreciation* and *perspective*. It also goes a long way in the complaint-reduction department.

Then there are the marvelous opportunities for discussion: talk about your own experiences. During bedtime reading with my older son, we would read a few pages of great stories of frontier living (I recommend the *Great Brain* series, *Shane*,

*Huckleberry Finn* and the abridged, kid-friendly version of *Tom Sawyer*).

Then as a fun treat I would show him YouTube videos of the crazy people of the sixties and seventies, people called hippies. There they are, dancing around and doing drugs and listening to music—wasting and doing nothing with their lives. They look so stupid.

It's a great lesson not only against using drugs, but about purpose, and how these same people hated America, and how many of them ultimately just died from the drugs. But they thought they were doing something so wonderful for the world. What was it they were actually doing to better the world? That wasn't very clear. I told them how my own dad said how easy it was going to be for me and my generation to do well, since these losers wouldn't be competing with me for jobs. He was right.

Here are suggested other conversations:

*Dad (watching yet another protest against capitalism on television, with his son): Wow, look at all those complainers. I wonder how they got there?*

*Charlie: I think they got there in cars, right?*

*Dad: Yes, but capitalism created the car. So they can't be complaining about cars, I suppose.*

*Charlie (beginning to catch on): No, I guess not! Maybe they're complaining about their clothes, their iPhones, and everything else they're using there. But wait—that can't be because capitalism invented those, too, right?*

*Dad (nodding, and smiling): Yep, you're absolutely right. Hmmm… Maybe they think socialism is a better way to go. I mean it <u>sounds</u> nice. Being "social" and stuff.*

*Charlie: So what does socialism mean?*

*Dad: Well, Charlie, it has nothing to do with being social, let's start off with that. Basically, it tells everyone that whatever money they make, they have to give almost all of it to the government, and then the government will provide most of the services they think you need—education, hospitals, food, even toilet paper. They also want to control how everything is made—telephones, TV shows, bicycles, toys, whatever.*

*So these guys think that's a nice way to live. Sure, you won't have any money to travel or buy any fun stuff for yourself, but it feels good for a while. There was this great leader of England, and you know what she said? "The problem with socialism is that sooner or later, you run out of other people's money."*

*Charlie (smiling and chuckling): That's smart.*

*Dad: So tell me, Charlie, what would you do if you made a lot of money and someone told you that you had to give almost all of it to the government?*

*Charlie (thinking): I wouldn't like that. That's just not fair.*

*Dad: Do you think you might move to a country which allowed you to keep a lot more of your money?*

*Charlie: (smiling). Yes, that's obvious, Dad! I would definitely move ["obvious" is a word Charlie just learned, and he likes to use it].*

*Dad: I think so, too. Or think of it like this: you do well in school. You get straight A's in a class. But the kids who don't study as hard complain and say that you should share your A's with them. They say whatever the average grade is of all the kids in the class, that's the grade everyone should get. They say that will make everyone equal. But will you study as hard?*

*Charlie: Heck, no!*

*Dad; Oh, and another thing: if you don't participate in or support the government programs, they'll put you in prison. In some "socialist" countries, they'll even kill you.*

*Charlie: What? That sounds crazy. (Pointing to TV). So why would they want that for themselves?*

*Dad: Oh, if you ask them, they think socialism works in other countries, like Sweden, Denmark, and Norway. But there's one problem with that argument.*

*Charlie: What's that?*

*Dad: They're not socialist countries. Some of them tried socialism, but they quickly saw how stupid it was and went back to being capitalist. I guess these protesters didn't get the news.*

*Charlie: (Laughs).*
*Dad: To be fair, some of them know that socialism doesn't work,*
*but they say it's because socialism has never been done correctly before.*
*They say this time, they'll get it right.*
*Charlie: How will they do it right?*
*Dad: Trust me, Charlie, they have no idea. It's done nothing but*
*kill and destroy or at least weaken the economy of every society that's*
*ever adopted it. But every society which has adopted it has always*
*started off with crowds and protesters just like the one you're seeing*
*there.*

*Hey, Charlie—remember a while back I told you about bad strang-*
*ers that might pretend to be nice to you and give you free candy if you*
*just go in their van?*
*Charlie: Don't worry, Dad. I would never do that.*
*Dad: Oh, I'm sure you wouldn't. You're one of the few smart ones.*
*But the people who are pushing socialism and convincing these people*
*you see there? They're just like those strangers in a van. They pretend*
*to give you all sorts of goodies if you join them. But then they take*
*away your freedom, forever.*
*Charlie: Being a socialist is stupid.*
*Dad: You know something? I think so, too, Charlie.*

The key is to know what America has done, all through its
God-based free-market system. The things I mention above
would simply not exist without America creating it and spreading it throughout the world. That includes the notion of ever-expanding freedoms, to ever-expanding groups of people. And
you have to know the history of socialism and how it's never,
ever worked.

Notice also how important it is to engage your child in
the process. Help him reach his conclusions. It's easy to do so
because you're just appealing to common sense and fairness,
something to which kids resonate *very* strongly. It helps that the
Left offers so much in the department of absurdities; something
which keeps increasing, like the constantly updated number of
burgers McDonald's advertises it's sold.

Here's another discussion:

*Mom (in car line to drop her girl at ballet class, seeing black, Latina and white girls getting out of their parents' cars): You know what's great? In America it doesn't matter what your skin color is or where you came from. All that matters is whether you're a good person, and what you can offer the world. Are you the best ballet dancer? Awesome! You can perform in the best theaters in the world. Are you the best at math and science? Great! You can help launch a spaceship to Mars.*

*Chloe: That's really cool.*

*Mom: It is, right? But you know something funny? There are people who will tell you that America is somehow the <u>worst</u> place in the world.*

*Chloe: Really? That doesn't make sense to me.*

*Mom: It doesn't, does it?*

*Chloe: One of my teachers, Ms. Osborne, said something really odd last week. She said that they made America to make sure slavery continued, in 1619. She said America was built on the backs of slaves....*

*Mom (concerned): Hmmm. What do you think?*

*Chloe: That's wrong?*

*Mom: Yes, very wrong. And I bet if you asked her to show you how that's so, she couldn't. And you can tell her America grew like crazy with jobs and inventions and making life better starting right <u>after</u> the Civil War—when there were no more slaves.*

*But you know what's funny? Do you know that almost everybody in the world would like to move here? Some would even risk their lives to come here! Everyone loves America, and loves it for its freedoms. Including people from Africa, Latin America, South America, and Asia.*

*So what do you think? Would they come here if they thought it was racist?*

*Chloe: Heck no!*

*Mom: It just wouldn't make sense, would it? And I'll tell you something else, sweetie: Slavery was <u>everywhere</u> in the world when*

*America had slavery. They make it seem as if America invented slavery. But it was because of America's Constitution that we were able to fight against slavery, and America was one of the first countries to make it completely illegal. We said: Every man and woman is equal in the eyes of God. So, after some time, we started questioning slavery, making it more difficult to own slaves. More and more states became free states that said no to slavery. Then we even had a huge war to end it everywhere in America! If America's main purpose was slavery, why would they go to war to end it?*

*Chloe: Yeah. Whoa.*

*Mom: The funny thing is that America's actually the least racist country that ever existed. Go to Japan, Germany, England, Spain, France, or especially many of the Arab and Muslim countries today, you'll see how they treat people who are different far, far worse.*

*Look, there are always some people who think that another group of people are not as good just because of skin color. That's just stupid, right? You might as well judge somebody based on their eye color or their height. What do you think?*

*Chloe: Yeah, I agree! It sure is stupid.*

*Mom: But in America, such people are very, very few. And it's actually America that's making it better for anyone who is different in any way. They're still not as good as America is, but America is leading the way. It always has. That's something your teacher probably just doesn't know.*

*Chloe: We're really lucky to be in America, I guess.*

*Mom: You know it! Now go on and have fun at ballet... And remember: a black girl like you can dance and compete with anyone here in America. Now go on and make your mom proud, okay?*

There are two key things to remember in all your discussions with your kids. Notice first that these conversations are between a parent and a *young* child, not a teenager. Again, as we discussed above, it is essential to get ahead of the issue way before teachers and social media start inundating them with their revisionist history and other woke agenda. If your child comes to you with the issues for the first time as he might have heard it from school, it might already be too late.

As I mentioned earlier in this book, note how I use the phrase *what do you think?* often. This is a "must" phrase you should use repeatedly in your discussions with your young children, for three reasons. First, it shows respect to your child for his thoughts and analysis. Children *love* this. They are *thinking* creatures, processing information every minute. Their little minds crave mental stimulation, much like they crave playing and running around, laughing, competition and other stimulation. They also appreciate respect like anyone else. *What do you think?* indicates respect for their opinions.

Second, this question engages them in the moment, and gives you feedback. He or she will be less likely to disassociate from the conversation or tune you out. Third, it develops their sense of critical thinking—something they will need if you want them to push back against the woke agenda.

Here's another fun discussion to have, while you're walking down the town boulevard, getting an ice cream cone:

*Dad: Funny to think what this place must have looked like a hundred and fifty years ago.*

*Stevie: What do you mean?*

*Dad: Well, for one thing, there wouldn't be any cars. There'd be a lot of horses, I suppose. And a lot of horse poop on the ground.*

*Stevie: Yuck! What else?*

*Dad (pauses): Well, what do you think?*

*Stevie (thinking): People wouldn't be flying around in planes above us. They wouldn't have air conditioning, and I don't think they'd have televisions and stuff.*

*Dad: That's good, yes!*

*Stevie: There wouldn't be playgrounds, basketball, or any computers or smartphones. There wouldn't even be lightbulbs!*

*Dad: Yes! Also, they'd only have one or two sets of clothes. They'd almost never travel anywhere beyond their city their entire life.*

*Stevie: But they would have ice cream, right?*

*Dad: Not so much, Stevie. Their idea of "fun" food would be jam on bread. And that'd be a super great treat for them, and very rare. Also, you know what's even more sad? Almost everyone you see now in front of you would be poor—like super-<u>duper</u> poor, barely able to live.*

*Stevie (amazed): Whoa! How can that be? Why did it change so much in that time?*

*Dad: One reason, and one reason only.*

*Stevie: Tell me, Dad.*

*Dad: America.*

And then Dad can explain America's unique God-centered market capitalism, with as much detail as I lay out from above as he likes.

There are *so many* teachable moments, everywhere you go. Even as you watch the news, stories and opportunities will present themselves, from a schmuck named Colin Kaepernick, a football quarterback who kneeled during the National Anthem, to the hero Jonathan Isaacs who eventually became the only one to stand for it. From the Antifa and BLM rioters who desecrate buildings, statues, and churches, and the students who shout down conservative speakers on campuses, to the movies about the brave soldiers and leaders from all America's past and present wars, *speak up and talk about them*. These are your opportunities. These are the small windows in time of impressionability in your children's younger lives.

They won't last forever.

## God and Evolution

This is the Big One. Perhaps it's the ultimate lode-bearing wall, without which everything would collapse. It's more foundational: Without God, there is no basis for distinctions. Without distinctions, there is no basis for civilization itself.

But distinctions are blurring and evaporating everywhere: the distinction between male and female is the most *au courant*. But there's also the ongoing battle to gut the distinctions between good and evil, right and wrong, criminal and law-abiding, adult and child, teacher and student, honor and shame, the holy and the unholy, Christmas, July 4, and Thanksgiving as meaningful holidays. Profane language and respectful language. Sexualized (and profane) clothing and decent clothing. Respectful entertainment and porn and other sexualized content.

There also seems to be the end of the distinction between America and the rest of the world. In the eyes of many on the left, borders should be no more. In a speech she gave to a Brazilian bank in 2013, presidential candidate Hillary Clinton said she "dreamed" of a "common market with open trade and open borders," saying that economic opportunity in the U.S. would grow as a result.

There's the destruction of all the distinctions I list above, and much more. I can't think of a single positive distinction that the Left *doesn't* want to minimize or destroy. Even election day has turned into a morass. It's become more of a season. When does it begin? Who knows. It's an undefined period of time in the year, like when you can wear white.

> Sally: Wow, the temperature dropped so early this year.
> Carrie: It sure has! I guess election season is upon us…
> Sally: Yes! And the season just seems to keep getting longer, doesn't it? I wonder if one day they'll extend voting all the way to Christmas.
> Carrie: What's Christmas?

## Identifying the Issue

You're seeing it and hearing it day after day: Believing in God is for fools who can't cope with the random and harsh nature of the universe. Science is what matters. The sooner we chuck Judaism and Christianity from our civilizational schema and move to the righteous path of Science with a capital *S*, the better. In fact, God as a concept is an anachronism and a crutch for all those who fear the cold realities of nature. It's an embarrassment to the advance of civilization. Besides, Christianity gave us the Inquisition, the Crusades, the priest molestations, the Salem witch trials, and oh-so-many other abuses.

Blah, blah, blah…

There will come a time, too, where schools will soon not only prohibit talking about God (thanks, to the 1962 *Engel vs Vitale* decision, see above), but will actively crusade in schools against God's existence. You'll start hearing stories of teachers pushing exactly this kind of activism by 2026 or so. Like so many other "movements," it will start off as a minor controversial topic, but will gain momentum, until the point Christians and Jews will find themselves in full Alamo mode. Not so much the Muslims. The Left fears the Muslims. They view Muslims like they view the Hulk. *You don't want to make them angry.*

If you're raising a skeptical eyebrow, ask yourself whether you'd have envisioned gay marriage to be the "civil rights issue of our time," or that schools would be pushing transgenderism. These were precursors of the demonization of God and faith: Destroy the pillars of marriage, family, and the basic tenets of biology itself.

The caustic language is already beginning: In early 2023, leaked FBI documents revealed a concerted effort to treat "Radical-Traditionalist Catholics" as domestic terrorists.[70] And don't think for a moment that by adding the precursor *radical-traditionalist* they recognize them to be only a minor "fringe" group exception. They will soon conflate all Catholicism to fall into this "radical" category, much the same way the Left often wants to lump all conservatives into whatever new extremist group it concocts for them ("Alt-right," "Tea-Party," "Q-Anon," "MAGA-Right," etc.) It'll toss *all* of them now into the great basket of deplorables.

At the very least, the Left will try to force conservatives to explain how they are *not* part of the extremist wing they've just manufactured.

> *Your liberal friend: Are you one of those Radical-Traditionalist Catholics?*
> *You: No. What are you talking about? I don't even know what that is.*
> *Your liberal friend: You guys are what's wrong with this country.*

The demonizing won't stop with Catholicism. It will extend to all Christianity, until the people who still do go to church on a more passive, I'm-going-because-I-think-that's-what-I'm-supposed-to-do-on-Sundays basis will eventually stop altogether. Why bother with all those boring sermons, and all that getting up and sitting down stuff? So that friends and co-workers can look at them askance and label them nut-jobs for doing so? *I'm all for God and Jesus and all that love stuff, but no thank you.*

Then they'll do it to the Jews, too. Then the Muslims... Wait, no they won't touch the Muslims. To the left, they're a righteous, besieged and oppressed minority. Plus, they hate Israel, so there's that. And like I said, you don't want to make those guys angry.

This is itself on the heels of lawsuits against believers for refusing to adhere to socially woke agendas, such as the Colorado baker refusing to bake a cake celebrating a gay marriage and, later, a transgender transition. Colorado courts later forced him to do the cakes. Or state and federal laws and mandates such as requiring the Catholic charity the Little Sisters to provide contraception and abortion services; or Christian colleges such as College of the Ozarks to allow boys "identifying as girls" into girls locker rooms and shower with them. The penalty for not allowing this? Massive punitive damages, six-figure fines for each violation, and payment of attorney fees.

This ain't your father's War on Christianity. Back in your father's day, it was just about stopping a kid from engaging in the heinous thought-crime of Christian prayer and whether he might spread that vicious contagion to others. It was also about Christmas plays which might, could, or possibly offend someone. It was whether you said *Happy Holidays* instead of that mortally poisonous verbal assault, *Merry Christmas.* Think of it as the difference between saying *African-American* and *the N-word.* (And don't worry, soon they won't even allow *Happy Holidays,* once they learn that *holiday* derives from combining the words *holy* and *day.* Oops. Someone call the girls at *the View.*)

Today, the war has extended beyond Christmas. Christians are the new Jews, suddenly awakening to the new fact that they've become the new outsiders. Polite society no longer wants anything to do with their dangerous and radical beliefs. And you know something? it's high time to get rid of them all.

That's exactly what the lawsuits and other intimidation tactics are all about. Some have even escalated to violence: Between January, 2018 and September, 2022, violent attacks against churches in America nearly *tripled* from prior years—420 incidents, including vandalism, arson, gun-related incidents, bomb threats, and more. At least 57 involved hostilities from pro-abortion activists between January 2022 and September 2022.[71]

Why are such attacks happening? Here are three reasons.

*Dwindling Church Attendance.* First, there are far fewer religious people than before, and Americans' membership in houses of worship continue to decline. According to a recent Gallup poll, US church membership remained near 70 percent for the last six decades of the 20th Century, but steadily declined to 47 percent in 2020 and is expected to continue declining. Worse, more and more Americans don't follow any religion at all. That percentage has grown from 8 percent in 1998-2000 to 13 percent in 2008-2010 to 21 percent as of 2018.[72]

The trend is likely to continue, with Gallup noting that church membership is strongly correlated with age. While membership for Generation X is 50%, it's just 36% for millennials and Generation Z.[73]

The latest generation's lack of attendance spawned even more apathy to attend church, and for those who remained, many turned away because the church seemed too judgmental, or didn't take on the correct political or social views. The pandemic shutdown of 2020-22 further broke habits and patterns of attendance, making it that much harder for pastors and other clergy to bring their flock back. The result? A new "flood" of churches available for sale.[74] As a result, the number of people who have little to no association with religion is growing like mold on bread. Christians are becoming a minority, which only emboldens the godless against them.

*Contempt.* This only adds opportunity for the younger generation to develop contempt for religion, and for the teachers among them to teach that contempt to their students. Worse, there will be fewer and fewer believing students to push back on anti-religious school agendas. Peer pressure will cause students to be less interested in religion, or at least in openly expressing their faith. Soon they'll join others who dismiss religion as backward, simplistic, and hateful.

It's a vicious self-feeding cycle resulting in many more of them, and far fewer of us. It's just a matter of simple math (although on the plus side, schools aren't teaching math, so they might not actually figure it out). Yet, as Hitler and his cronies did regarding the Jews in Europe, the Left will make it seem like Christians are everywhere, trying to suppress all those who don't think just like them. And they absolutely, positively, must be stopped.

*The New Cultural Hatred of America and Religion.* Along with this new-found license to dismember God and God's history, comes a breathtaking disrespect and contempt for faith, history, America, and civilization at large. Athletes kneel during the national anthem, and the rest of the nation follows like lemmings. After only a couple of years, athletes are reprimanded for *not* kneeling during the national anthem.[75] People receive pink slips for not sufficiently celebrating gay pride month.[76] The

United States requires all embassies abroad to fly gay-pride flags alongside the American flag—but naturally nothing reflecting pride in America, women, Christians, or Jews. Stanford University even proposes banning the very words *America* or *American*.[77] Finally, churches themselves—the ones still remaining out there—are facing cultural backlash and reprimand for failing to recognize the "science" of transgenderism and for rejecting same-sex marriage, birth control, and abortion.

Hence we see the massive uptick in the defacing and destruction of American monuments, churches and pro-life centers. It's the inevitable consequence of non-stop rage against civilization and against God Himself.

In the end, it's a numbers game. More of them, fewer of us, does not bode well for the continued vitality of our Judeo-Christian values.

There seems to be so much hatred going around for almost everything. By contrast, there seems very little to aspire to. Don't worry: I suppose the Left will let you choose from their list. But you'll notice it looks a lot like a very limited menu in a Soviet-era restaurant.

## Getting Ahead of It

You've talked about God and the importance of faith to your child. You've engaged with her about how there can be no freedom without Him, no civilization, no sense of purpose. You've talked to her about how God created the universe through the Big Bang, how life began through God—and how no one could ever re-create life out of inorganic materials. You've talked about the complexity of the human cell and the perfect symphony of the human body and its interacting organs, the perfection of the earth's atmosphere and earth's place in the solar system, and how none of these things could have come about randomly.

You've talked about how there can be no consciousness or free will without a creator who gives it to us. You've talked about how the world was like before the arrival of Judaism and Christianity: A world of brutality and lawlessness, where families didn't matter, and people bought and sold other people like horses or pigs. You've talked about how Judaism gave the world morality through the Ten Commandments, how it gave the world a sense of time, justice, and the sanctity of the individual. You've talked about how Christianity gave the world the concept of one Truth, created the University, the hospital system, the modern day school system, the modern version of the scientific method, and brought about the concept of free speech and modern-day limited government and freedom.

You'll need to let her know that there will be people who will tell her otherwise: Even some of her schoolteachers will say that there is no such thing as God, and that the universe, earth, life and intelligent life came about by itself. They'll also say that "religion has done more destruction and killing than anything else," and that Christianity wants to get rid of gay rights (if not gays altogether), keep women from working, encourage racism and antisemitism, and otherwise sideline anyone who doesn't accept Jesus as their Lord and Savior.

This will be her biggest challenge. Make sure she's ready. Better yet, make her impervious. Make her that Hurricane Hunter plane traversing the massive storm without getting rocked at all.

There are two approaches here to getting ahead of it. First, showcase the complexity of the universe and life, and second expose the silliness that life and the creation of the human being could have happened randomly.

## Lies, Damn Lies, and Probabilities

I spent a good deal of my parenting life talking to my kids about odds. I find it to be one of the most effective ways of understanding issues in general.

I remember once talking to the kids while we drove past some big building along one of the busier streets of our town: "Hey guys: What are the chances that a brick will fall from the top of that building right on top of our car?"

They look at each other. "Not very likely."

I egg them on: "Okay, but give me a fraction: Is it one out of two, like the flip of a coin, or is it like one of ten, hundred, or whatever?"

They start guessing. The older one says something like one out of 10,000.

"Great," I say. "I don't know for certain, but that might be about right." Then I continue: "But now what are the chances that instead of a brick falling down, it's the principal of your school, Mr. Cohen, and he's playing my favorite song, *Hey Jude*, by the Beatles on his piano while he's falling. Also, he's wearing a clown outfit while doing so with that rainbow hair wig thing? What are the chances that all that will happen in that combination, exactly as I just said it?"

My kids look at me preposterously: "Zero," they say. "There is no chance of that at all."

"Nope," I retort. "There is in fact a chance. It'll be a very, very small chance, I'm sure, but there is always a *chance*—no matter how ridiculously small—that exactly that scenario might play out, so long as it doesn't defy basic reality."*

---

* Some readers may have heard of the similar concept of the "infinite monkey theorem," which proposes that, given enough time, a monkey randomly striking keys on a typewriter will end up typing out a perfect copy of the play *Hamlet*. I'm not so keen on using this, since the odds of the universe, earth, and life creating itself just so is far less likely than that. Additionally, the visual is not as engaging for kids. Most kids don't know *Hamlet,* for one thing. For another, it's best to invoke scenarios which bring in people and things they can relate to in their own lives. Hence my use of Principal Cohen from my kids' former school. Such scenarios make the absurd probabilities more tangible, and less abstract. Then they themselves can create other scenarios. It also activates the child's imagination much better this way.

At this point, the kids are intrigued. We continue to throw out more craziness as we drive, each scenario more goofy and more preposterous as we do.

Don't worry, I'm going somewhere with this.

I do another probability game with them, this time a bit more practical: I'm taking my son to his swim practice, which is about four miles away. As we start our drive, I ask him what the odds are that the car in front of us is also going to the same swim practice with their kid. He knows that it's highly unlikely, so he says "pretty small. Like, really small."

I agree with him, but as we get much closer to swim practice, I ask him about the car that's *now* in front of us. What are the odds that *that* car is going to our swim practice? He says it'll be the same, but he sees me already shaking my head.

"We're closer to it, so there are fewer possibilities that this car will turn a different direction than the one before." So I explain the odds are therefore a bit better.

And so on it goes, and he begins to see the pattern. By the time we get into the garage at the building for swim practice, and I ask him the same question, he says "very high." Is it a 100 percent? No, but much, much more than before.

Here's the point: such numerical and probabilistic thinking helps you see the realities of God. I don't want to get ahead of myself here, but I'll present you with this intriguing thought: I *do* believe in God for the same reason I *don't* believe in gambling, drinking to excess, or taking drugs.

How can I put these things together? The odds.

After my Principal-Cohen-on-the-piano-playing-Hey-Jude-in-a-particular-clown-suit scenario, I don't talk with my kids about the chances that life came about randomly. I just want them to have fun. But the process gets them thinking in terms of numbers and statistics; it engages that muscle for them. They begin to see that most things in life involve choices and decisions, and their likely consequences. Incidentally, you'll find this way of thinking useful when you'll be talking to them later about the consequences of engaging in reckless sex, taking drugs, and voting democrat.

And it's useful to talk to them this way about God. How so? People assume that belief in God is something people just fall into. But I think that's a bit of the tail wagging the dog: It's better to first figure out whether there's a Creator at all. And for that analysis, we first need to wonder if anything we see and know about the universe, the earth, and life could have happened by itself. In short, like the Principal Cohen scenario, what are the probabilities of *that*?

There's a lot to factor in, all at once: The perfection of the universe and the Big Bang's precise combination of chemicals and atomic structure (any other combination would have led to a gaseous universe, with no formation of anything), the Earth's placement in the solar system, the presence of Jupiter (to suck away asteroids that would otherwise impact Earth), the moon's presence (not only necessary for essential tides, but to keep the earth on its axis), Earth's circular orbit (instead of elliptical), our unique ozone layer... and so on, and so on.

And there's a lot more information we learn as time goes on, including the extraordinary interconnectedness among all these things.

Here's one of the great ironies: Contrary to the atheist mantra that science will disprove God, the exact opposite happens. That is, the *more* science we learn, the more absurd it is to suggest that our universe, the earth, and life itself came about on its own.

Oops.

And now the money shot: What are the odds of the universe ever formulating in as life-compatible a manner as it has? The physicist Lee Smolin has calculated that the odds of life-compatible numbers coming up by chance to be 1 in $10^{229}$ (that's 1 followed by 229 zeros). These odds are *in addition to* the similar astronomical odds of the earth forming in the right part of the universe and galaxy, the right placement in our solar system, with all the other necessary perfections that make life sustainable at all.[78] *

Scientists have modeled what the universe would have looked like if any single one of its constants—the strength of gravity, the mass of an electron, the cosmological constant—had been even slightly off by even the smallest infinitesimal amount. What has become clear is that, across a huge range of these constants, they had to have pretty much *exactly* the values they had for life to be possible.[79]

Now, what are the chances of *just* life itself ever forming spontaneously (even assuming the universe is as it is)? Evolutionists themselves acknowledge the chance of even a simple protein molecule forming at random in an organic soup would be only one in $10^{113}$. Yet mathematicians will dismiss any event that has one chance in just $10^{50}$ as essentially never happening.[80]

Oh, and to give you an idea of the staggering size of the improbability: The number $10^{113}$ is more than the total number of atoms estimated to be in the universe.[81]

And those odds are just the beginning. One has to then *also* factor the astronomical odds that this newly formed self-created life would then reproduce itself, evolve itself, and evolve to intelligent life with free will. It is virtually impossible to figure such odds, but they are no doubt even more astronomical than the previous odds I mentioned.

And one last thought: for *all* these things to happen, *all* these astronomically small fractions have to be multiplied *with one another*, leaving a fraction so small that to speak of it as a real

---

* Incidentally, it is because scientists know the absurd improbability of these odds of random generation of the universe, the earth, and life that they concocted the concept of a "multi-verse." Why? Because if there are infinite amounts of universes, then the odds that at least one of the universes will have the perfect qualities that ours has increases dramatically. But there is no evidence of a multi-verse. It was created solely as a tail-wagging-the-dog effort to explain away the inconvenient finely-tuned universe (yes, *one* universe) that we have. In addition, as explained in *Goff, supra,* there's an additional problem: the odds with each universe is always the same. It doesn't get better because of the existence of more universes. For example, no matter how many times you flip a coin the chances that it will land heads at any one time, each time, is *still* 1 out of 2. As Goff's title correctly puts it: Our improbable existence is no evidence for a multiverse.

possibility in any manner simply insults the intelligence. It is the equivalent of throwing thousands of boxes full of Scrabble letter tiles from the top of the Freedom Tower in New York City and expecting them to land in just such a way so that they spell out the entire series of the *Harry Potter* books, all in perfect order from start to finish with the exact right spacing and paragraph breaks—multiple times, all in a row.

Or as likely as my kids' principal teacher, Mr. Cohen, falling from a building playing *Hey Jude* on a piano while dressed in a clown suit with that rainbow wig and landing on the top of my car while I happen to be driving by with my kids, a thousand times in a row. All by pure chance.

Now you know why I play that game with my kids.

## Evolution and its Discontents

Today, it's culturally genetic to hear about schools teaching evolution and rejecting the concept of Intelligent Design.* You've likely heard about the Scopes Monkey Trial (1925), during which a teacher was tried for the illegal act of—gasp—teaching Darwinism in school! The poor man lost, resulting in the ever so shameful prohibition of the teaching of evolution in schools, for decades. There was even a movie about it, *Inherit the Wind* (1960), featuring Spencer Tracy and Gene Kelly, among other serious actors of the day. In the movie, the fix is in against embattled Science, and the poor teacher *who just wants to teach science that's all,* never seems to catch a break: Every time he calls a scientist or other authority figure to help discuss Darwin's theories, the judge sustains the prosecution's objections and forbids the testimony.

---

* Many confuse (perhaps intentionally) the concepts of Creationism with Intelligent Design. These are very distinct concepts. In summary, Creationism argues that God designed the universe and our world in six earth days. Intelligent Design argues something far broader: that there is a design to the universe, with intelligence behind it. What or who that designer may look like is a different story, without regard to whether it follows the biblical narrative. Atheists often conflate the two, perhaps so as to dismiss the argument of any apparent design in the universe.

Poor Science, losing to those backward yet dangerous Southern hicks. Will truth ever prevail? What can we do to avoid this retreat to exclusionary ignorant religious madness from happening again?

It wasn't a real trial, mind you. In realty, it was just a lighthearted "show" trial the town of Dayton, Tennessee had concocted to get attention and boost business for the town. However, the ACLU wanted a test case and advertised for a teacher willing to be a nominal defendant in that staged prosecution.

The volunteer ended up being a man named John T. Scopes. Scopes was just a physical education teacher who had only briefly taught biology as a substitute. There was never a danger of him going to jail.[82] Think of the whole endeavor like school kids putting God, America, Christopher Columbus, or Anthony Fauci on trial for their alleged wrongs against mankind. It can be fun for debate practice, but you're not about to collect on the judgment (well, we're still hoping about Anthony Fauci).

Evolution versus Intelligent Design. It's been a raging debate for almost two centuries. But problems kept arising—problems you should point out to your kids often. The theory goes something like this:

> Billions of years ago, chemicals randomly organized themselves into a self-replicating molecule. This spark of life was the seed of every living thing we see today (as well as those we no longer see, like dinosaurs). That simplest life form, through the processes of mutation and natural selection, has been shaped into every living species on the planet.[83]

The theory rests on three foundational principles: First, that the DNA of an organism will occasionally change, or mutate. Second, the mutation is either beneficial, harmful, or neutral. Third, as mutations spread over long periods of time, they cause new species to form.[84] *So simple! Why can't you just get on board with the program?*

But there's a problem. Actually, there are many, many problems. Among them are:

(1) *No evidence in the fossil record.* There has never been any fossil showing a true missing link between apes and man (the purported ones you learned in high school, like Piltdown man, were fakes), let alone from any one species to another. But like the political left who pushed the Russia Collusion hoax, the scientists pushing Darwinism weren't eager to admit they were wrong, and so you were left thinking links existed.

In fact, quite strangely, the fossil record instead nearly matches the general order of the appearance of living forms found in the Bible's book of Genesis. As physical chemist Donald E. Chittick comments: "A direct look at the fossil record would lead one to conclude that animals reproduced after their kind as Genesis states. They did *not* change from one kind into another. The evidence now, as in Darwin's day, is in agreement with the Genesis record of direct creation. Animals and plants continue to reproduce after their kind. In fact, *the conflict between paleontology and Darwinism is so strong that some scientists are beginning to believe that the in-between forms will never be found.*"[85] Emphasis added.

Wait. Rewind. *The evidence is in agreement with the Genesis of direct creation?* Oops.

Then there's the related fact that the animals arrived in almost precisely the same sequence as Genesis describes it.[86] What are the odds that the Founding Fabricators of the Bible happened to guess *that* correctly? Remember those Scrabble tiles now.

(2) *The Cambrian Explosion*: Scientists unearthed a treasure trove of fossils of numerous species from 540 million years ago, all of which inexplicably arrived at the same time (first-time animals with mineralized skeletal systems). There was no progressive, methodical development from more primitive to more complex.[87] Scientists hid this information for decades, while the evolution mantra gained traction and became accepted as scientific reality. I suppose it's the evolutionist community's version

of the Hunter Biden laptop; an annoying reality that just won't go away.

(3) *Irreducible complexity.* Biological systems like the inner workings of a cell, working with the organs, and each organ working together with the other, cannot function unless all of their individual parts are present and working together. Those parts have to have arrived and worked together *at the same time*, not randomly one at a time, waiting for its necessary counterpart components to arrive one day, by happenstance. Example: the space shuttle didn't organically come together, first with one wing, then another that happened to be the exact same (but mirrored) sized shape, then an engine (and all the parts thereof), fuel, windows, protective casing, etc. That would be absurd. We know that NASA put them together as one whole project, with each part in reference to the other, to work together. Virtually every part was dependent on and contemplated the related functioning of the others, at the same time. The same is even more true with a vastly more complex machine—the human.

(4) *The impossibly extraordinary complexity of life, and the massive amounts of time necessary to effectuate each of the "mutations" called for by evolution.* No one explains how long it takes to go from one evolutionary change to the other (let alone to become another species). Is it 20 years? 200 years? 2 million? The planet is only 4.5 billion years old, and life as we think of it (multi-cell organisms) only started 900 million years ago. Reptiles started only 400 million years ago. I know we all overestimate how much we can do in one day, but evolutionarily speaking, this is squeezing a *lot* of activity into very little time.

(5) *The evolutionary process is supposedly random, but we see no evidence of the randomness.* Do changes all proceed in the same, positive direction? Where are the fossils of animals with three legs, or just one eye? It seems evolution was extraordinarily efficient, despite it being absolutely random, with very few detours. It's like driving across the United States without ever

using a map, compass, stars or sun but always choosing *just* the right roads to get there—and in record time. Oh, and you're blindfolded the entire way.

Evolutionists nevertheless continue to assert that no intelligence factored into the creation of life, despite these and other problems. In addition, there are many things that evolution simply can't account for, at least in terms of survival of the fittest: free will, consciousness, language, beauty, storytelling, art, music, spirituality, a sense of obligation to the past and to the future.

Oh, and humor.

*Billy: Did you hear about John? He just died.*
*Joe: That's awful. He must not have been funny enough.*

Dismantling evolution is also fairly easy because it must fully explain absolutely *everything* we see through a lens of randomness. There can be no interference or hint of design. To do that, the evolution advocate has to provide consistently plausible *random* explanations for *everything* in the universe and *everything* in the generation and adaptation of life. Otherwise, the house of cards must fall.

With all this background, you've now got ample ammunition to move to the next step—laughing at it.

## Laughing at It and Dismissing It

When talking about those who insist there is no God, always revert to rule number one: *Young kids love absurd things.* And for those who preach atheism or evolution, there's plenty of absurd to go around.

You need only point out so many of the things I reference above, and you'll lock it in in their minds: Things that are sophisticated and complex, especially the human mind and body, can't develop out of nothing. As Fred Hoyle famously put it, the chance our lives emerged randomly is about the same as a tornado sweeping through a junk-yard full of wires, nuts, and bolts, and inadvertently making a Boeing 747.

I suppose that's a great way to start. But you can do this with everything. Everywhere you look, point it out and say how nice it was created out of nothing.

*Dad: See that building over there with the red awnings across the street?*

*Sammy: Yes.*

*Dad: It's so cool how it came out of nowhere. Totally random.*

*Sammy (giving a funny smile): Dad, are you joking with me?*

*Dad: Oh to hear it from our evolution friends, a bunch of things got together and formed naturally. It must have been really amazing: Just the right amount of wind, sand, water, and all sorts of other … gobble-dee-gook, I suppose… came at just the right moment and WHAMO… You got yourself a building right there! … And same thing for all those other buildings around it, I guess. Man, isn't nature just awesome.*

*Sammy (beginning to get it). And those lampposts right there. And those busses. And those airplanes in the sky!*

*Dad (laughing with Sammy): Why not? If they think people came about totally randomly, well then why not buildings and busses and all that stuff? Oh, the wonderful world of atheism. Anything's possible!*

*Sammy: Those people don't make sense.*

When driving with the kids, ask them the most absurd scenario they can think of (like their Principal Cohen falling from the building playing piano in a clown suit, landing right on top of our car). They'll come up with awesome things. Kids *are* creative. And then let them know that the chances of *that* happening are far greater than the universe coming out of nowhere, the earth forming as it did, or life happening as it did. In fact, no matter how absurd their scenario might be, let them know they're not even close and they'll just have to be even more crazy.

"Even more!" you'll say. And they'll oblige.

Here's a fun dialogue you can write with your child so he can understand the concept of irreducible complexity, and to attack the idea of pure random evolution. Maybe you can even act it out in front of the family at dinner:

*Bob: Howdy, neighbor! What a nice new car you got there!*
*David: Thanks, buddy! It came together a while ago.*
*Bob (confused): What do you mean, "came together?"*
*David: Well, you see it was a slow process, Bob. At first, I just bought a wheel. Then I thought, you know what? I'm going to get another wheel, just for fun. Sure enough I guess I went crazy and got myself another two. Then at another point, I got myself a tail pipe. Then a windshield wiper, and so on. I didn't really have any idea that they might go together, but then one day I opened up the garage door, and they all just came together. … It's kind of weird now that I think of it.*
*Bob: Wait, you just built this out of just random things you got?*
*David: Well, no, to be honest, it kind of built itself. And what was really cool is that they all knew their particular role somehow.*
*Bob (more confused than ever): What about the sound system, the air conditioning chemicals, the spark plugs, the windows?*
*David: Funny, I guess I just got all the right things and they all fit and worked together. Now that you mention it, I guess I got kinda lucky.*
*Bob: Why didn't you just buy a whole car from the dealership?*
*David (confused): Wait… That's a thing?*

Here's a fun one you can use on the fly, with regular house chores. Mom sees her son Todd going up the stairs to his bedroom:

*Mom: Todd, your room is such a mess! You really need to clean it up.*
*Todd: I know, I know. I'll do it. But can I wait until tomorrow morning?*

*Mom (thinking): I tell you what. I'll do you one better... According to our evolution friends, you can wait a few million years. It'll just clean itself up!*

*Todd (smiling): Wow. I love it! Anything is possible with those guys!*

*Mom: Yes indeed. (Her face changes to one of concern). I suppose there is one problem, though.*

*Todd: What's that?*

*Mom: We don't have a few million years.*

Last one, dealing with free will:

*Dad: Oh, what a great day I had today! I punched my boss in the face.*

*Jamie: What? That's crazy! You can't do that!*

*Dad: Why not? I couldn't help myself. It just happened.*

*Jamie: Wasn't your boss really upset about that?*

*Dad (waves the kid off): No. Once I explained to him that there's no free will and so I can't be held accountable, he was good with it.*

Never let an absurdity go to waste.

## Transgenderism

Once there was a king. He ruled over his people in a fair and respectful way. The people loved him and obeyed his very reasonable edicts.

Being the king, he had his own water well. Everyone else shared a separate water well just outside the city walls. One day, the water well for the people became tainted with some strange substance. What it was, no one knew, but soon a horrible thing happened: The water made the people crazy. They started doing the most absurd things: they walked on their hands, sang when they meant to just talk, laughed when they were sad, and used dirt to clean themselves. They even started voting democrat.

The king quickly noticed something was amiss. Even his guards and noblemen were talking gibberish and offered gifts to the horses and pigs, whom they thought were their new overlords.

Naturally, this state of affairs troubled the king. He tried reasoning with everyone. He made demands upon them to behave normally. He ordered his guards to arrest the next person to act strangely. But the guards weren't listening. In fact, no matter what he did, people just laughed at him as though *he* was the crazy one.

He tried and tried to figure out a solution to the problem, but he soon realized the situation was hopeless. He came to the horrible realization that he ruled a kingdom which had gone insane.

But he *was* still their king.

So what did he do? He went out the city walls, walked to the people's well, and lowered the water pail into the well's water, and pulled the pail back up, full of water.

And then, after taking one last look around, he drank from their water.

My mother told me this tale when I was nine years old. It obviously stuck with me. It didn't seem to relate to anything we were talking about on our drive together to my swim team practice. But there it was.

Maybe she wanted to let me know that in the future, people would be saying crazy things. Yes, it would be tempting to drink the water. But don't. Just don't. Anyway, that's what I hope she meant.

Because when it comes to the transgender movement, everyone seems to be drinking from the tainted water well.

# Identifying the Issue

## How Did we Get Here?

The transgender movement seemed to just descend upon us, moments after the *Obergefell* decision of the United States Supreme Court in 2015. We simple folk were still cleaning up other people's confetti and litter from the ticker tape parade celebrating same-sex marriage on our Main and Elm streets, when the transgender commandos swooped into our schools, locker rooms, sports, and even our language.

It was much more sudden, too. Where gay marriage developed over more than ten years, transgenderism came in full force, like German Panzer division tanks and Messerschmidt bombers in a furious German *blitzkrieg* style attack.

And just like the allies in WWII, we had no idea the attack was coming. Within only months of the first mention of "transgender rights," we were told to not make assumptions about anyone's pronouns, to let men into girls' locker rooms and restrooms. Within only a couple of years, the transgender activists had completely taken over the gay rights movement. In fact, gay rights suddenly seemed passé. They weren't even an aggrieved minority anymore. Gay rights were now *so* 2014. In one episode of *Modern Family*, the gay character Cam tries to argue for better treatment as a high school football coach, reminding the principal that he's gay. The school principal responds, unphased: "Gay? That means nothing anymore. Now if you were transgender, *that* would be something."

How did it all start? There were discussions of transgender "rights" for decades—whatever that meant. Was it the right to vote, to an education, to free speech? Oh, you mean the "rights" to go into the opposite sex's bathroom and locker rooms and participate in their sports and wear women's clothing at the office. Got it.

The movement started as early as the early 1920s, when the term "transexual" was first used. From there, it went to hormonal therapy in 1949, and then the movement battled in the courts, getting more awareness of the existence of transgendered people.

Mind you, it was and remains a dysphoria—that's a mental disorder. Just like a gaunt anorexic sees herself in the mirror and thinks of herself as fat, a man might see himself as a woman, and vice-versa. In fact, the American Psychiatric Association still sees it as a mental disorder. The *Diagnostic and Statistical Manual of Mental Disorders, Fifth Edition, Text Revision (DSM-5-TR)* provides one overarching diagnosis of gender dysphoria with separate specific criteria for children and for adolescents and adults. It defines it as "a marked incongruence between one's experienced/expressed gender and their assigned gender, lasting at least 6 months," and manifested by at least two of six listed desires, perceptions, or convictions.[88]

But as this is only a mental disorder, how does a doctor justify responding to it as a *physical* disorder, with massive hormone injections, castration, or mastectomies? The problem is in the mind, not the body. To treat it as a physical issue would be like arguing we should just get rid of all guns as the answer to stop crime.

But that would also be an absurd comparison, I suppose. No one would ever argue that.

## Numbers, Numbers, Numbers

What's absolutely fascinating about this is that few ask the following question: *Just how many people are out there with a true gender dysphoria?*

It's a fair question, isn't it? If there were only, say, 1,000 people in *all* of America with a disability, for example, would it be right to require all businesses to commit to the Americans with Disabilities Act (ADA) and force them to reconstruct every single business building with ramps, toilet stalls, handicap parking spots and otherwise, all for the sake of that tiny subset of people?

So what is the number of people with true gender dysphoria who need our understanding and sympathy? To hear it from the woke crowd, you'd think every third person was confused about his or her gender and sexuality. It's so prevalent, in fact, that we should all change our language in its most foundational forms—pronouns and all our other word choices, definitions and assumptions of sexuality and gender.

But it's not even close to one out of three people. For males, it's 0.005 percent to 0.014 percent of the population, and 0.002 percent to 0.003 percent for females. That's according to the vaunted DSM-5.[89] Assuming a population of 330 million, that translates to … wait for it … 6,600 individuals on the low end and 46,200 on the very high end. Taking an average for both men and women, *that's 26,400 in the entire United States.*

That's it. Let me repeat that: *26,400 in the entire United States.* Not 26.4 million. 26.4 *thousand.*

So let's get this straight: we're asking the entire country to view each other differently, revamp our entire language and culture, literally change the way we introduce ourselves (the preferred "her/he/zhey" etc. game), ensure inclusion in every government office and college campus, and dedicate hours each day in our schools to re-orient thousands of years of basic understandings of two sexes, so that we can appease this incredibly small group of people.

To get some perspective, here are the relative proportions of other minority groups:

Blacks: 12%. That's approximately 42 *million.*

Hispanics: 20%. That's approximately 63 *million.*

Native American: .7%. That's approximately 2.3 *million.*

Jews: 2.4%. That's approximately 5.8 *million.*

Gays: 3% to 7% of the population (depending how one defines "gay"). That's 9.9 to 20.3 *million.*

Legally blind: .03%. Approximately 1.3 *million.*

Hard of hearing: .3%. Approximately 10 *million* persons are hard of hearing and close to 1 *million* are functionally deaf.

Color-blind people: 3.7%. Approximately 12 *million* (7 percent of males, and 0.4 percent of females. But the overwhelming majority of these are men, so no wonder no one cares about them.)

Gluten-intolerant people: 7%. Approximately 23 *million*.

Eating disorders: 9%. 28.8 *million* Americans (meaning an eating disorder sometime in their lifetime).

Left-Handed people: 10%. Approximately 33 *million*. You may think this is an irrelevant issue, but it's not easy being left-handed. Here are just some of their issues: Scissors, school desks, handwriting, sports, can-openers, guitars and other musical instruments, credit card swiping, cameras, tools, crossword puzzles, spiral notebooks, computer consoles, and zippers. This is to say nothing of the "discrimination" in language: *Gauche* is French for "left." *Sinister* is Latin for "on the left side." By contrast, good things are associated with being on the right: *Dexterous* means being on the right side, and *adroit* means "the right way." In French, the very word for the law (*le droit)* means the "right." And of course, *right* also means "correct."

Not convinced yet? Well, you may like to know there are twice as many Eskimos in the United States as there are transgenders (approximately 55,000), and about 40 times as many Gypsies (up to 1 million).

You can go on with other afflicted and aggrieved groups (diabetics, epileptics, hemophiliacs, migraine-sufferers, etc.) All of these groups are each *vastly greater* in numbers than those with gender dysphoria and who have very *real* troubles navigating their world all their lives—I mean beyond the horror of not being able to expose one's penis in front of women in locker rooms, which admittedly is a suffering *no one* should ever have to tolerate. No one.

But we don't suggest everyone must learn to read braille, lest the blind feel excluded. We don't insist everyone bring a sign interpreter with them wherever they go. We don't demand every restaurant offer a gluten-free section. We don't encourage left-handed people to write their papers from right to left if that'll make them feel better. We don't replace all traffic lights with color-coded signs and manuals with symbols. "The fight for color-blind equality is the greatest civil right of our time!" said no one.

*Jerry: Life is so rough for those poor transgendered folk. We need to change all our bathrooms and locker rooms so that everyone can feel comfortable.*

*Frank: You are so right! And I think we should also change all traffic lights and signs to include symbols, for those who can't distinguish colors as easily.*

*Jerry: You're being absurd.*

Somehow, we allow this one *exceptionally* tiny group of people to upturn our entire world—and for what? That they don't feel comfortable in the restroom and locker rooms designated for their own sex. Never mind the discomfort and worries of *actual* girls and women who have to accept a person with a penis in their restrooms and locker rooms. Those feelings are not important right now. Not only that, if we don't bow to their demands, we are "phobic" of them.

The argument I've heard is that transgenders get savagely and routinely beaten in the locker rooms and restrooms, what with everyone hating on them so much. Yet I have yet to hear a single story of such an event. Even if such events did happen, say five times a year, it would not be enough to justify the guaranteed discomfort girls and women feel every time a male just struts into female locker rooms and restrooms.

## Rapid Onset Dysphoria

The Left—or whoever is in charge of the new hysteria—seems to understand that there are only so many "real" gender dysphoric people out there. To inflate these numbers, they turned it into a social cause, encouraging everyone to walk the walk, and more importantly, talk the talk. Through social media and other agitprops techniques, the number of teenagers identifying as trans, queer, or non-binary exploded, especially among adolescent girls. They seized upon teenagers' natural desire to fit in, to feel special.

The effect was almost immediate. Suddenly, where gender dysphoria used to be mostly a male thing, it fully reversed starting around 2007. Among adolescents seeking transgender medical interventions, biological females began to outnumber biological males by a factor of 2.5 to 7.1.[90] "Rapid Onset Dysphoria" became a new term, although the good people at *Psychology Today* were quick to dismiss the phrase, on account of its stunningly accurate summation of the phenomenon.

Even the World Professional Association for Transgender Health, which supports medical interventions for children who believe they're transgender, acknowledged a sudden surge in "nonbinary" identities in its latest guidelines. It also noted a growing number of patients who had never experienced gender dysphoria in childhood. It acknowledged that both were signs of possible peer influence. As the organization's head, Dr. Erica Anderson (himself a transgender) put it: "Adolescents are very susceptible to peer influence, so to suggest there can be no influence on young people is preposterous and flies in the face of everything we know about teenagers."[91]

The result? Childhood gender dysphoria diagnoses rose *50 percent from 2017 to 2021,* with most of it happening in 2020 to 2021.[92] The schools have been a primary encourager. Suddenly, those who didn't belong to a socially acceptable aggrieved or victim class had a lifeline: "non-binary." They could now bathe themselves in all the new attention in a brand new pool of their own making.

## Transgenderism Becomes the New Fascism

Why do we get so cataclysmically terrified about the transgenders (*if you don't allow them to get "gender-affirming" surgery, they'll kill themselves!*), but have proper perspective when it comes to those with color-blindness, Celiac disease, and Turrets syndrome, especially considering the considerably smaller presence of transgenders? Why does the left insist that we must not only accept transgenders, but celebrate and applaud them as if we were all at a North Korea rally for Dear Leader?

Then there's the audacity of leftist teachers, professors and politicians openly promoting *actual violence* against anyone criticizing the transgendered takeover of our culture. There were calls for a "Trans Day of Vengeance" to support transgender rights—as though transgenders (remember: 26,400 of them at most in the entire country) were facing throngs of phobic skinheads who beat them senselessly—every day! *Now, it's payback time, oh yeah.*

*Trans Day of Vengeance.* Surely *that's* a call for a mostly peaceful protest, if there ever was one. If you think the title suggested violence or were concerned because those pacifists known as Antifa were organizing it, you'd be wrong. You'd also be one of those irrational "phobics" who hate democracy, science, and people who just want to *love*.

Never mind that Antifa had scheduled this Day of Vengeance just one day after a female transgender horrifically slaughtered three adults and three fourth graders in a Christian school in Nashville, Tennessee in late March of 2023. Somehow, the left-wing media converted that particular school shooting to make it so *transgenders* were the real victims. The fact that the killer herself had wanted specifically to kill Christians because Christianity didn't accept that there were more than two sexes, and a girl could choose to be a boy? That's not important now. What *is* important is that you know that transgenders are four times more likely than "cisgendered people" to be victims of violence.[93] *That's* what should be your take-away from that particular incident, and nothing else. Oh, and we should ban guns.

Yes, it was unfortunate those people got in the way of the bullets she was firing, but they were collateral damage in the service of allowing the killer to express her important and justifiable transgender rage. Plus the victims *were* Christians, after all, so they were expendable when you consider the larger picture.

The ever-apologizing media seemed to have emboldened the hostile tone. A professor at Wayne State University brazenly proclaimed, "I think it is far more admirable to kill a racist, homophobic, or transphobic speaker than it is to shout them down." (Although he prefaced that comment by making it absolutely, positively clear that he did not advocate violating federal and state criminal codes.[94] Apparently, there's an exception in those criminal codes to murder campus speakers, so long as those speakers are of the *phobic* persuasion).

*Cop arresting and cuffing a perp, caught in the act of murder: Ok, Freddy, it's the slammer for you. Juries don't take too kindly to murder in these parts!*

*Freddy: But the bastard was a phobic!*

*Cop (embarrassed, uncuffs him): Oh, sorry. Off you go. Please accept my apologies. Please don't sue the city.*

Likewise, Josselyn Berry, assistant to Arizona Governor Katie Hobbs, posted a social media meme showing a picture of a determined-looking woman toting two guns. Her clever caption? "Us when we see transphobes." She thoughtfully posted it just hours after the Nashville attack.[95]

Just one week after that attack—when you thought cooler heads might eventually prevail—Democrat minority whip for Wisconsin, Karlee Provenza, tweeted a picture of a maniacal-looking elderly trans-woman with an assault rifle. Its caption read: "Auntie Fa says protect trans folks against fascists and bigots!"[96]

I wonder what message she intended? *Whoa, those transgenders sure are tough hombres…. I mean mujeres. I mean…. Oh, you know what I mean!*

There's more. Now you can say almost anything when it comes to sex or sexually deviant behavior. Teachers have been caught showing elementary school kids how to use dildos. One teacher lay down on a desk and lifted her legs high to the sky while bringing an actual dildo close to her vagina for visual and more realistic effect (I'm guessing a mere diagram or drawing wouldn't have sufficed). Then there's the teacher having students read a story about nine-year-olds watching grown men pleasuring themselves. In yet another incident, high school students were asked to grade how comfortable they were with anal sex. Another asked kids to write down which classmates they'd like to be intimate with, and how so—anal sex, oral sex, kissing, licking of ears? Another teacher required kindergarten students to draw a picture of where the best place in their home was to masturbate.[97]

But why are you complaining? It's just the usual "Four R's" any parent would want his kids to learn in school: reading, writing, 'rithmetic, and rear-door sex.

Then there are the drag queen story-hours. Schools, libraries, and community centers can't seem to get enough of dancing men wearing gobs of absurd makeup and skimpy and sexual women's clothing, reading *Go Dog, Go* to young children. In some cases, children are encouraged to touch these men in inappropriate areas of the body. If these were instead *actual* women dancing provocatively, giving lap dances, and removing clothing in front of child onlookers, someone would certainly go to jail. Child Protective Services would visit the parents.

Why is all this happening? To desensitize kids to overt depictions of adult sexuality. As the people who just think better than us at *Psychology Today* put it, such events will help trans and sexually confused kids see that they are normal. The *real* danger is in *not* exposing them to "other templates as they begin to sort out their feelings about who they authentically are."[98] So it's all good, there's no chance of harm, and don't be a hater.

> *Activist: We need to teach children to understand transgender-ism, and all its many facets, and that a boy can be a girl if he wants to. This is a new dynamic that is critical for their well-being and for society as a whole.*
> *Parent: Great! So can I ask that we teach about the importance of God to your child?*
> *Activist: Whoa. Let's not go crazy.*

This is all dangerous territory. Exposing young kids to sexual content has enormous deleterious impacts upon mental health, life satisfaction, and later sexual behavior and attitudes. Yet the push to impose such shows and readings on children, as well as encouraging masturbation and pornography use, continues.[99]

Keep in mind that some parents are knowingly bringing their very young children to these readings, so one might say there's a demand for this. The fact that parents are willingly doing so doesn't justify the practice, nor make them any less guilty of child abuse.

Everyone's getting on the you-better-celebrate-or-else train. Sports teams and other organizations have been expected to show their allegiance to the cause. The NHL was asked to sport rainbow-colored hockey sticks and jerseys, with gay-flag rainbow colored lighting displayed before the games. But goaltender James Reiner of the San Jose Sharks refused to participate, which practically elevated him to the status of Soviet refusenik.

The LGBTQ+ community in San Francisco descended upon him, saying *not* putting on the pride-themed jersey "sent a dangerous message." According to Suzanne Ford, president of San Francisco Pride, members of her community "have suffered under the yoke of people thinking and acting like that. And we have been afraid of it. … I'm not going to stand for it."[100]

> *Charlie: Can you believe all the new hatred against Jews?*
> *Bret: I know, people are not wearing Stars of David and not waiving Israeli flags when we demand them to. Also, they refuse to put our "Jews Rock!" bumper stickers on their cars.*
> *Charlie: It's so oppressive.*
> *Bret: Yes. We have suffered under that yoke for too long.*

Huh? We're actually *oppressing* gays and transgenders for *not* wearing clothing or otherwise *not* messaging our active support? It's no longer good enough to just *stop* the oppression (whatever that is). What if I don't wear the clothing they want me to wear, as often as they like? Am I oppressing someone if I don't wear it all the time? Who decides when I may *stop* wearing the pro-trans messages you require? When I go to sleep, may I wear pajamas that don't have a pro-trans message? Asking for a friend.

Why not require people to wear positive messaging about Mormons, Jews, Armenians, Tibetans, Seventh-Day Adventists, Jehovah's Witnesses, vegans, and women with curly hair? Each of them has faced challenges. Why not force people to wear "Black Lives Matter" shirts every day and require permanent "Love is Love" lawn signs or risk social cancellation or even violence?

Is this not a form of oppression itself? Better yet: Is this not a form of terror?

And how is this not similar to Mao-era Chinese paramilitary Red Guards punishing their citizens because they didn't carry or couldn't properly quote from Mao's *Little Red Book*?

## Answering the Big "Why"

Why do the media and the left persist in pushing the transgender lie in total disproportion to the numbers? Surely, they must know there are so few truly gender-dysphoric people to justify such an upheaval of society, much less of history and common sense.

Why turn our world around transgenders, but not the other groups I reference above? Why, for that matter, are they going well beyond "understanding" the plight of transgenders but *encouraging* young people to embrace deviant sexual behavior in all its forms? By contrast, no one is pushing your kids to write left-handed or experience being blind.

There is only one reason: Their hope is to break down the distinction between male and female. If they do can that, Christianity and Judaism will collapse. To them, it will mean the hastening of the end of God. As more laws force recognition of transgender rights, and as they get more kids to hold basic understandings of the differences between male and female in contempt, churches and synagogues will find themselves at odds with the new "science" and the new "basic" understandings of civil liberties. They will feel forced to accept the new reality of many genders and the transmutability among them — or face government closure and public ostracization.

That, coupled with forcing recognition of gay marriage, while gutting what "family" means, allows the left to hollow out religion, particularly its favorite target, Fort Christianity. They know they can't succeed (yet) in a full-on frontal assault on the fort, so they are pursuing its destruction indirectly. Think of it as cutting off the enemy's supply lines, and watching it starve. Then they'll dig underneath and invade from there. They don't have to breach the fortress itself.

The Great Forced Acceptance is already happening. In early 2023, Oregon's Department of Human Services refused a woman's application to adopt a child from the state's foster care system because she would not affirm to "respect, accept, and support the gender identity, [and] gender expression" of any child the department might place in an applicant's home. The woman could not agree because of her faith, and the department denied her application.[101]

Also in 2023, the 7th Circuit Court of Appeals determined that a school's pro-transgender policy outweighed a teacher's religious rights to not refer to them by their preferred nouns and names.[102] Also in 2023, a large and angry pro-transgender mob assaulted swimmer athlete Riley Gaines in San Francisco because she didn't believe men should compete in women's sports. The police did nothing.

A New Mexico attorney proclaimed to teachers in a teacher training video that "parental rights end when you send your kids to public school."[103] A California State Assemblywoman proposed a bill which would allow therapists to send a gender-confused child to a residential shelter facility without parental knowledge or any legal procedure.[104] In Washington, the legislature passed a bill allowing shelters to take children away from their parents for not consenting to gender transition procedures on their child.[105]

Churches will soon face the loss of their tax-free 501(c)(3) status because they don't fully embrace the LGBTQ+ agenda. Very soon, activists will compare churches to those who had fought for the separation of blacks and whites.

We are being played. The new transgender dogma has nothing to do with science. Nor is it about improving the lives of trans individuals. It is about destroying God. The left knows that the male-female distinction is the lode-bearing wall that props up all Judeo-Christian faiths, and civilization itself. None of those other things (sight, hearing, food allergies, Turrets, Celiac, etc.), are cornerstones of civilization.

That is why transgenderism is their battlefield. To them, this is their moment, akin to Waterloo, Yorktown, or Normandy.

The bad guys are very, very interested in destroying civilization. And all they have to do is get you to drink the water.

## *Laughing at It and Dismissing It*

This is both incredibly easy to laugh at, and incredibly hard. On the one hand, you've got the basics of being a boy and being a girl. Kids start noticing the differences between ages three and four. On the other, the schools are unrelenting in trying to convince your kids that there is no such thing as gender (at least the two genders binary "paradigm").

You're dealing with the Goebbels' theory on lying: Tell a lie often enough, and people will believe it, regardless how absurd it may be. Or, as Voltaire more ominously noted, "Those who can make you believe absurdities, can make you commit atrocities."

The drip, drip, drip of the lie, hour after hour and day after day in school is hard to combat. That's why you need to start fighting this lie as soon as you can. And that starts with making your boy feel awesome about being a boy, and your girl feel awesome about being a girl.

Yep. It's that simple.

*Dad: Vic, what do you think? You like being a boy?*
*Vic: Yeah!*
*Dad: Boys are AWESOME. That's what I say!*
*Vic (Nods head. Proud.)*
*Dad: Tell me all the cool stuff boys like to do.*
*Vic (thinking): We like to go FAST. We like to blow stuff up and then build them again! We like to ride bikes and get in the mud and get dirty!*
*Dad: Totally!! You see all those cars and buildings and roads all around us?*
*Vic: Yes.*
*Dad: All built by BOYS. That's what we do!*
*Vic: Boys are the BEST.*
*Dad: You know it! And girls, what do they do? They just like flowers and dresses.*
*Vic: Girls are so silly.*

Remember this: Every kid wants to belong to something, to feel special about who they are—yes, even the vast majority of regular boys and girls who are *not* confused about being a boy or a girl. They need to celebrate and be proud of their "boy-ness" and "girlness," too.

It's so easy to help them along. Just have simple discussions like the one above. Certainly, among the children who gravitate toward the social contagion of transgenderism, I would guess they weren't raised with much "pride" in being a boy or girl. The parents likely just let the kids float down the social river, letting the currents tug and pull at them wherever they might take them.

Notice in the dialogue above how I not only propped up boys, but made fun of girls (I'll do it in reverse soon enough; don't panic). *It's completely okay to do this.* It's actually developmental for a boy to appreciate his boyness, and to see girls as "stinky." It is too much to expect a boy to know all the nuances of girls at such a young age. They need to understand first who they are as boys, and then once they do so, explore the world of girls later. Same thing in reverse.

Each of us know this intuitively: when we men grew up as boys, we just wanted to hang out with the other boys, catch frogs, make daring jumps off cliffs and throw rocks at each other. When I was a boy, we had a communal lake in our neigh-borhood. In the winter, we boys would all skate on it, with no adult supervision. How did we know the ice was thick enough to skate on? We threw a huge rock on the ice. If it didn't crack too much, we figured we were good to go.

Anyway, we thought playing with girls was weird. If you liked a girl, it meant that you liked girl things, too. You were like, you know, a *traitor.*

It's less so in reverse (a little girl liking a boy), but they still make clear that they don't "get" boys and they don't want to. In the end, they preferred dolls and all the other girl things. And boys were the stinky ones.

Anyway, as promised, here's a similar discussion with your daughter.

*Dad: Katie, what do you think? You like being a girl?*

*Katie: I sure do!*

*Dad: Girls are AWESOME. That's what I say!*

*Katie: (Nods head. Proud.)*

*Dad: Tell me all the cool stuff girls do. I don't know, 'cause you know – I'm a man, so....*

*Katie (proud to explain something to her dad she knows better than him): We like dolls and looking nice. Playing house with our toys. Playing with baby animals. Baking with mom. We like making things look pretty. Unicorns and horses. We like to dress up.*

*Dad: Oh that is so cool! I like that! Girls are cool. Girls and ladies make the world so much nicer to live in.*

*Katie: Thank you. Yes. They sure do!*

*Dad: Just look at all the cool patterns and beautiful things in houses and stuff. Look at that garden! You think a man would figure that out?*

*Katie (absurd look): Heck no.*

*Dad: You know it! And all the other nice stuff in life, too! All the beautiful clothing and designs, the nice fancy restaurants we all like, the designs in the inside of homes. Girls do that!*

*Katie: Yeah! Girls are awesome.*

*Dad: And boys, what do they do? They just like to eat dirt and throw rocks.*

*Katie: Boys are crazy.*

*Dad: Except for your brother and grandpa Joe and grandpa Marty, and Uncle Felix, I suppose. So some men are okay, right?*

*Katie: Yeah, they're okay. And don't forget you, too!*

*Dad (smiling): Thanks, sweetie!*

Notice in this dialogue how the dad asks his daughter to explain something about girls because he, dad, is a man and can't know. It enlivens and engages her because she's providing information that he admits he can't know.

Again: *Girls love being girls, and boys love being boys.* Their boyness or girlness is something they know well, so if you're the opposite-sex parent, let them "teach" it to you.

In today's world, you're expected to reject that distinction, let alone "pride" in that distinction. You're supposed to tell your boy about the greatness of girls while insisting no one is different than the other. Yet the embracing of one's sex and its differences from the other is one of the most important moments in a child's development. And therein lies a problem: We're insisting there are no differences.

As a father, you may feel awkward because your wife or other women in your life might get upset with you for saying boys are great, or have some qualities that are "better" than girls. So you self-censor. Likewise, for you mothers, your feminist friends keep asking you to punch up on the feminism thing, so you feel this obligation to prop up girls. You worry that any celebration of boys suggests a suppression of girls. You feel guilty about letting little Tommy be "all boy," and even worse about encouraging Abby to play with dolls.

Keep in mind, this "girls and boys are the same" garbage started way before the woke agenda supersized it and injected it with steroids. If you want your children to have a healthy identity in their gender, then all that garbage has got to stop. *Let it go.* Go with what you've always known to be true: *boys and girls are very, very different.* It's just not right to start teaching your girl that boys are just as good or vice versa, or that some boys like girl stuff and vice-versa.

Stop. Just stop. It's like talking to your child about God for the first time but also telling her that same moment how you don't know why God let the Holocaust happen. You would never do that. Everything in its appropriate time.

But not with these woke guys. They want you to learn about anal sex, oral sex and masturbation at the same time as they teach you about holding hands and kissing. They want you to see men prancing around as women as much as possible, and expose your children to all the strange fetishes out there.

But have you noticed? Lost in all of this is any discussion even of having boyfriends or girlfriends, or any long-term real "relationship" of any kind (even the same-sex kind). Relationships aren't as important as how you chase your orgasm. Because, as I developed more fully in my book *Rise of the Sex Machines*, if it's all about pleasure, then there's no obligation to anyone else. It's only about you. And don't even mention marriage. Marriage should be taken out to the woodshed and shot, horrific patriarchal system that it has always been.

It's all about the sex. Hold the relationships. That's what they're gunning for.

So talk about the madness. This dialogue may be the most important one you'll ever have.

Again, talk about it in absurd terms. And the woke mob is certainly dishing the absurdities in spades for all to see.

Like the American government in the early days of WWII needed only to show Hitler's own propaganda films to Americans to reveal how evil the Nazis were, we need to do the same. Unveil the evil of how the woke are trying to destroy civilization's most basic distinction of male and female, through transgenderism.

In short, far from shying away from it, expose it for the madness it is.

*Mom: Can you believe it? There are some silly people out there thinking you can just change into anything you want.*

*Bertrand (perplexed): What? What do you mean?*

*Mom: Sure! They're out there saying that a boy can be a girl, and a girl can be a boy.*

*Bertrand: That sounds weird. Boys can't be girls!*

*Mom (putting her hand to her chest): See, that's what I thought, too, but the silly people are out there saying you can! So I thought: Wait, if a boy can be a girl, then why stop there? I can change into anything else! So last Tuesday, I was an ostrich. It was real fun for a while, but then I decided to be a freezer. Then, for about an hour or so, I became George Washington. But then I remembered I had to get coffee with my friends at Starbucks, so I came back.*

*Bertrand (beginning to get it): I want to be a frog!*

*Mom: Now you're talking! Tomorrow, I'm thinking of becoming a car like Lightning McQueen in that movie. That way, I can get to places real quick instead of walking.*

*Bertrand (face lights up, suddenly realizing something): WHOA. You'll be like the Transformers!*

*Mom (realizing that herself): Wow… You're so right. Why didn't I think of that? Transformers are REAL!*

*Bertrand: Yeah!*

*Mom: But seriously, Bertie… What do you think? Do you think a boy can be a girl… like, ever?*

*Bertrand (giving her a look): Mom, you know I'm not crazy, right?*

*Mom: Well, there'll be some teachers and others at school who'll tell you that. But just because they say something, doesn't make it right, right?*

*Bertrand: I'll just tell them they're silly.*

*Mom: Great. That sounds good to me!*

Think positively about it all: The transgender movement offers opportunities galore for fun conversations. It's a river which feeds many streams. One of the arguments we should always make is about the "pride" thing: Gays and trans people should be "proud" because of who or what they're attracted to, or how they identify. But if you want to express pride about all the accomplishments of America, Western Civilization, or Judeo-Christianity? Sit down, big fella.

Here's a sample:

*Dad: Hey, remember all those things we mentioned that America did that was so great?*

*Mila: Yep! America is awesome!*

*Dad: I agree. Pretty proud to be an American! Also, I'm pretty proud to be a Christian. And Jews should be proud to be Jews.*

*Mila: Really? How so?*

*Dad: Well, let's see. Together, Jews and Christians gave the world the concepts of time, justice, law and order, cleanliness, charity, science, hospitals, and even the concept of school for all kids. Oh, and the Ten Commandments!*

Mila: *Whoa, that's awesome. We should have a "pride" day for that!*

Dad: *You'd think so, sweetie… But no.*

Mila: *What? They have gay pride and trans pride. What did <u>they</u> do?*

Dad: *That's a good question, Mila. But the important thing is that they sure are proud of themselves.*

Mila: *That's not fair to Christians and Jews, though!*

Dad: *Good point, sweetie. Look around you: almost everything you see around you—buildings, police, courthouses, schools, cars and all that kind of stuff—all of it's here because of Christianity, Judaism and America. That's why we're conservatives: we appreciate what those things have done for us. And we're part of those things. WE did this. And when you're older, maybe <u>you'll</u> do more of those great things.*

Mila: *Conservatism builds stuff. Liberalism tears it down.*

Dad (couldn't be prouder): *I think I have something in my eye.*

Here's a discussion you can have about how the trans world activists want us to change everything about our civilization, and how small they are in number.

Mom: *Hey, Evan, you know how your friend Sakai is a Buddhist from Japan?*

Evan: *Yeah, it's like a different religion, I think.*

Mom: *Yes, it is. It's a nice one, too. But what if Sakai said everyone should stop saying Merry Christmas, or we should all stop celebrating all our holidays because it's not part of his religion or his country?*

Evan: *That wouldn't be right. He's in <u>our</u> country! He can't tell us to change who we are! I wouldn't ask him to change everything in Japan for me.*

Mom: *Absolutely. And what if, say, there was a special group of people—only like 10,000 of them in all of America—who believed* *saying the word "America" might turn them into tiny zombie giraffes. So now, because of them, you can't say the word "America" to <u>anyone</u>.*

*Evan: No, that would be silly. They should get used to us, not the other way around. And that's such a small number of people!*

*Mom: Exactly! Well you know there's a very small group of people out there just like that! They want us to change all our language because they don't know if they're a boy or a girl, and they'd get very upset if you call a boy a "he" when he wants to be a "she."*

*Evan: That's not right.*

*Mom: I don't think it's right, either. Not at all. And they're a tiny, tiny group of people. There's like this many of them (makes a gesture with her index finger and thumb). Tiny! But they want us to never say "boys and girls" or "ladies and gentlemen" anymore, just "children" or "people." And they don't want you to use the words "he" or "his," even if you look like and <u>are</u> a boy. You're supposed to ask them ahead of time.*

*Oh, and if a boy dresses up like a girl, you're supposed to pretend along with him that's he's a girl.*

*Evan: That's like super, super duper crazy. I would never do that. Never.*

*Mom (confident that her job is done here): Good to hear that, son… Good to hear that.*

Again, notice in all these dialogues I emphasize engaging the child in the talk, to ask him what *he* thinks. Secondly, keep in mind that he's listening for direction from you. Lead him there, yes, but ultimately let him to know at the end of the discussion how you come out on the issue. They *do* seek your approval, and they want to know they're on the right track.

Yes, as I said before, this *is* indoctrination. But it's also the right thing to do. You're the parent; it's your job to share your values and give them direction. Everything you do is "indoctrination," one way or the other. And whether you want to or not, you have no choice. The schools and so many other forces are out there trying to indoctrinate your child using every technique imaginable.

So don't feel guilty about it. *They* are the monsters. Not you. Never forget: It's a battle for your kids' minds. America was very reluctant to get involved in WWII, but ultimately, they had to throw themselves into the fray. And just like America, you've now got to get into the fray for your kids.

Because this is also a very real war.

## All the Other Things

Of course, there are many other topics to conquer. We can speak at length about describing each such issue, getting ahead of each issue with your kids, and then laughing at and dismissing them, one by one. But you've got the techniques down by now. Below are many additional issues of the day, with some general quick ways to deal with them:

1. Guns and gun-control (if we outlaw guns, only outlaws will have guns. Also, guess who liberals want to send into dangerous situations? Social workers);
2. The meaning of free speech (hint, it's not about whether someone might offend your feelings);
3. Affirmative action/ race-based preferences (do you think it's fair that someone gets a better deal just because of their skin color or their nationality? Isn't that racism?);
4. Israel (it's the size of New Jersey, not Texas as many people think; it's also the only real democracy in the entire middle east, is virtually the most tolerant to gays in the world, and far from being a so-called "Apartheid" state has minorities of all kinds—including Arabs—in all political, judicial, business, medical and other walks of life);
5. Merit and excellence in competition (is it fair that daddy or mommy work so hard to have this nice house and then someone who doesn't feel like working takes it

from them? Is it fair that you worked so hard to be the best on the basketball team or get the best grades and that everyone gets the same award or grades?);

6. Modern feminism (has it helped? Where are they in support of real women in locker rooms and in women's sports? Is there something good about the differences between men and women? Do women have to be the same as men?);

7. The demonizing of boys and "toxic masculinity" (without masculinity, there will be nothing ever built, no sustained fight against evil, and no protection of the family. Boys eventually become men and we need good men);

8. How the world responded to the Covid pandemic and the oppressive mandate of the vaccine (the 15-days to flatten the curve that lasted two years, they were wrong about virtually everything [masks, wet-market pangolin theory, vaccines are 100% effective, the shutdown would prevent deaths]);

9. Marriage and family (they don't want marriage, fathers, or the traditional nuclear family, but what would happen in a world without marriage, fathers, or the traditional family?);

10. What sex means (it's a special bond between a man and woman, and primarily for making a family. An additional interesting note for parents: it's extremely *unhealthy* and even dangerous if you have too many partners but extremely *healthy* and completely safe when you have a *lot* of sex with the same partner, especially in a marital bond);

11. The need to have children (what would happen if no one would have kids? We need *more* people [the good kind] on the planet, not fewer);

12. Abortion and the so-called right to choose (kids have strong opinions about this and develop a natural aversion against abortion when they realize that it involves killing little babies. "Do you think it's right to kill a baby because

you don't feel like taking care of it? Why do women call it a baby if they want to keep it, and a fetus if they want to get rid of it? Has anyone ever been to a Fetus Shower? And such a mother can give the baby up for adoption: hundreds of thousands of couples who can't have children would die to be able to adopt such a baby!").

The techniques I lay out above apply the same way to each of these additional issues: First, know that they're out there, and realize the schools will bring them up. Then describe and explain each of them as *you* see it, well before they even get to school. Mock the leftist viewpoint (because they are all worthy of mockery). Finally, engage your child by asking your kids what they think of the issue, and gently guide them in the right direction. In the process, tell them also what some teachers and administrators at the school or among their friends may tell them, and how they can ignore that.

And always, always laugh at the absurd. Laughter is not only the best medicine, but the best shield against the madness.

# CONCLUSION

I've written this book because we're at war. The problem is that people don't realize it, or don't *want* to realize it.

There are many kinds of war. There's the World War II kind, where we defended against an impending threat to our existence. There are the Korea and Vietnam kinds, where we sought to contain the spread of evil. There are also wars within a nation, such as rebellions and civil wars. You may think I'm going there, that we're in a civil war of sorts. But I actually don't believe that.

There are revolutionary wars, too—to shackle off the perceived evils of a former dogma, such as was the agenda of the American, French, or Russian revolutions. You might think I'm gunning to make that point, too, but I don't believe that this is a revolution, either.

This is a different kind of war. It's not so much a war of ideas, as it is a war to *end* ideas. In this war, there's nothing anyone is really aspiring to, such as we aspired in WWII (the quest to push back and ultimately destroy fascist evil), the Civil War (the quest to end slavery), or even the American Revolution (the quest for freedom). It's not even the run-of-the-mill expand-the-empire land grabs, such as the ancient wars of Rome, Greece, Mongolia, Babylonia, or Persia.

Unlike all such wars, this is a war to *destroy* civilization. It's a war to obliterate all ideas, particularly distinctions, without any meaningful plan to replace them with something better. It's a war to force descents: descent into barbarism, ancient rituals and primitivism, nature-worship, even tribalism. Our enemies seek a return to a more clan-like existence, where family as we think of it is no longer the cornerstone of society. The "village"—whatever that means—is much more important. Sex and marriage with anyone or anything is fine, and equity, massive wealth transfers, and selective law enforcement are the new paradigms.

The State should decide what is moral (but only after close consultation with self-appointed experts). Self-satisfaction, including drugs and alcohol, are all encouraged. Whatever perception you want for yourself, you go with it. Indulge yourself.

Yes, you hear the likes of Bernie Sanders and many others pushing for socialism, but even they must know socialism can't work if there's no social framework to actually put it *in*. After all, there is no "marriage" anymore. There are no borders. Law enforcement is collapsing. Leftist politicians and judges seem almost to be advocating for greater criminality. There's even a push not to have any more kids; it's not too clear what kind of civilization they expect—socialist or otherwise—if there are no people to run it.

So expecting something even as unworkable as socialism to work is like expecting a building to stand when there are no concepts about what construction even *is*, much less uniform codes to ensure safety and stability. To make the metaphor even more apt, they won't even know where or how to get the lumber, concrete, wires or plumbing for that matter. That would require work.

The point is that they don't really want socialism. They don't want *anything*. Everything that's now happening around us—the attack upon chivalry, masculinity, the distinction between male and female, marriage, family, hard work, America and the roots of Western Civilization—is part of a larger quest to just burn the mother down.

We're all in the first stages of this war—the stage where very few people actually realize that war has already descended upon us. Much like we didn't see Hitler was already warring with us before he made his first pushes into Austria, Czechoslovakia, and Poland, and much like China is now warring with us without firing a shot but overtly spying on us and owning our land and infiltrating our industries and politicians, leftists have been successfully overtaking and demarcating critical turf: the media, social media, sports and entertainment, and of course our educational system.

If you don't see this theme happening all around you, you are either too busy to deal with it, or too frightened to deal with it. I've realized this from my many talks with most parents who have to come to me for help with their children. They want to pursue legal action against their kids' school, or fight school boards who turn a blind eye to pornography and push to normalize mental illness in their kids' education.

But we need to take responsibility. This is *our* fault. We should be no more angry at the leftists doing this to our kids than we should be angry at vermin and weeds in our gardens when we don't maintain them, or angry at criminals who commit crime when we don't enforce the laws. Destruction and corruption of the mind is what leftists *do*. They'll stop only if we push back on them.

The good news is that pushing back isn't that hard. The recent rejections of Stanford University's absurd proposal to not say *American* (among other words), the rejection of Bud Light for its use of an obnoxious transgender person as its spokesperson, and the disaster of Disney's woke let-me-shove-gay-scenes-in-your-kids'-movies, prove how easily it is to counter the woke agenda. But we actually have to *do it*.

The reason why this has been happening at all is because, as Steve Jobs warned, we've ceded all authority to schoolteachers and administrators. We've made them think that we don't care. We didn't teach values as we should have because we didn't

really value our values ourselves. We believed in general principals of patriotism and God, yes, but they were amorphous aspi-
rational concepts that we didn't really know, let alone know
how to articulate.

Then we kept telling ourselves that one woke encroachment
after another was no big deal (no prayer allowed in schools, no
intelligent design education allowed in schools, foregoing the
Pledge of Allegiance, pushing for same-sex marriage, allowing
kneeling during sporting events). We came to expect teachers
and schools to be the ones teaching values to our children. We
let these monsters into our kids' minds because we figured the
teachers knew best and wanted the best for our kids.

And it doesn't help when the country seems to care less and
less about patriotism, God, community or even having children.
According to a 2023 *Wall Street Journal* poll, just about only a
third of the country say such things are "very important" to
them, down from about two-thirds who said the same in 1998.
The only value that has grown in worth to Americans is money,
which jumped in importance to 43 percent of those polled, compared to 31 percent who said the same in 1998.

Sad, no?

Well, we have our work cut out for us. That means having
to re-instill the values we've lost. We can no longer assume it's
going to seep into kids through social osmosis. On the contrary,
the left is trying to impose a new osmosis of its own.

So instilling values and history is our oar to row now; we
cannot and should not rely on anyone else. We should act as if
there are no other people out there who support our values, as
if the kids must rely entirely on us. We can no longer afford the
luxury that things will work out. There are just too many evil
forces out there.

Figure out what you value yourself first. If you truly love
God and America, you'll need to understand it won't come to
your kids passively, as it may have come to you when you were
a kid. A new wind is blowing, and you have to tack against the

wind instead of having the wind behind you. Yes, your own parents didn't have to deal with this, but this is the new reality.

You'll need to identify the issues of indoctrination, get ahead of them, explain them, and then laugh at them. Then, and only then, can you dismiss those issues in the minds of your kids. In this book, I've given many sample dialogues any parent can use, but you can certainly tailor them to your own style.

Remember the keys you must use. Humor is essential. Show respect for your children and engage them in the issues. Ask them to give absurd scenarios of their own. And remember the one mantra that should play in your head over and over again: *kids love laughing at the absurd.* Give it to them. There's plenty of absurd to go around.

In the beginning of this book, I analogized what is happening in the schools to kidnappers who invade your home and steal your kids from you. I said it was worse than that: you're actually delivering your kids *to* the kidnappers, on *their* turf. You have no idea what the monsters are doing to your kids for six or more hours a day. It's like leaving them with a babysitter who's a pedophile, day after day.

But just like you know that you can't always be with your kids every moment, you can still prepare them for most situations. We already do it to some extent: We warn kids about "stranger danger," and that just because an adult tells them to do something, they don't have to do it—or even respond to them. We tell them about drugs, and that someone might offer them drugs, but that drugs will destroy their lives. We tell them how to respond to bullies with words, and sometimes how to punch back.

We prep our kids because we know our kids will encounter most if not all these situations. And the time has come when we need to prep our kids against the agenda we know will happen in their schools—not so much from their fellow students but from their teachers, administrators, and school curricula. I've already had to talk to my own kids about the possibility that a teacher will tell them "Don't tell your mom or dad. You and I know what's best for you, right?" Wink, wink… It's a terrifying but real prospect.

I've also told my kids that it's okay to challenge the teachers. To advance their woke agenda, many teachers exploit the impressionable nature of their young students. The teachers know our kids don't have the same critical thinking abilities we adults do. Teachers can also wield the power of grades and passive social stigmatization (*Oh, did you notice that, everyone? Tommy thinks there are only two genders! That's fine if his religion teaches him that, I suppose. But we here at Obama Elementary believe in <u>Science</u>. Who here believes in actual science? Raise your hand!*)

I'm not saying your kid has to be obnoxious. But I am saying that you need to arm your kids with certain key points that they can use. When it comes to evolution, your kid can respond: "What about the Cambrian explosion? And how come no one has found missing links from one species to another? There should be tons of them!"

On global warming: "I hear what you're saying, but how do we know the temperature measurements and calibrations are 100% accurate over the past few decades? Who is recording them? How come government subsidies always go to those seeking to prove global warming, but not challenge it? Why did all the experts say we were all going to die of global *cooling* back in the seventies? Also, Al Gore was wrong on every one of his doomsday deadlines…."

On the greatness of America: "What country has created more inventions than America? What country gave the notion of free speech to the world and what country spread freedom to so many other countries? What country is less racist than America? If America is so awful, why does everyone want to come here, and why does everyone want to copy everything we do in clothing, music, movies, technology and just about everything else?"

You'll be surprised how proud the kids will be when they best the teacher. You should know all these counterarguments and rejoinders. I've developed a lot of them in this book to discuss with your kids, so that it will be natural for them to engage and defend their values, their country, and Judeo-Christian civilization.

It won't even be that hard for them. Most teachers have never really faced meaningful challenges to their nonsensical platitudes. Their ideas will collapse once your kids push back, like popping a soap bubble with the slightest touch. The worst that'll happen is that the teacher will be upset with your kid because he made her look ignorant.

Important: tell your kids you'll always have their back. If little Charlene finds herself in the principal's office for challenging a teacher or anyone else, let her know not only that you'll be there with her, but if she stands up for what's right (America, God, actual science), you'll give her a reward—and make it a "big" reward, one that Charlene will really appreciate. Show your pride for what she did by talking to the whole family later about it at the dinner table. When your own conservative friends come to your house, let them know—with your child present—how she pushed back at school. She will beam with satisfaction when your friends shake her hand in support.

Remember the good news: you have the advantage. Your kid is with you from birth. As soon as they are able to communicate, have fun talking with them about silly things: *Can people make the sun rise? Can I turn into a cow whenever I feel like it? Do airplanes just make themselves?* Then have fun talking about the awesomeness of God, America, and Judeo-Christian civilization, and all their contributions. Talk about the silliness of socialism and how it has never worked, and how cool capitalism is.

I've said it's easy. Why? Because you have all the facts, logic, and history on your side. You don't have to memorize much, because most of what you'll be talking about with your kids is right there in front of them, as plain as the color of their eyes, gravity, and yes, their genitalia. You just have to *do* it.

And I can't stress this enough: *Get to them while they're super young:* as soon as they're able to understand the most basic things—I mean the age when he still gets excited about the garbage truck passing by, or when she still thinks she can be a unicorn-princess.

Why so early? Because your school system and all the media are looking to mold the wet clay of your kids' minds at ever-earlier ages in their lives. You simply *have to be there before the teachers get there.* First in time wins.

Beyond children's inherit love of the absurd, we've also talked about children's natural need for your approval. They not only will follow your lead, but they *want* to follow your lead. They look to you to lead them. They're expecting you to show them boundaries and to make sense of the world. Help them do just that by giving them meaning to the issues of the day, explaining not only what is what, but what is right, and what is wrong.

You don't have to be savage about it. You don't have to refer to anyone who doesn't believe what you believe as "stupid." But you can say what makes sense to *you,* and why you disagree with others' ideas. Yes, you can even say you think the others' ideas are silly. Because they are.

Finally, to those who claim that all this amounts to indoctrination of your child: This is what parents *do.* In fact, indoctrination is your number one job. You teach your child your religion (indoctrination); love of your country and why your country is the best (indoctrination), and why your music and sports team are the best (that would be Tim Montana and the Patriots, respectively) (also indoctrination).

And that's okay. Others can demand that right when *they* do all the baby-carrying, feeding, diaper-changing, doctor visits, monster-under-the-bed consolations, clothing and toys, bedtime reading, driving to school and after school activities and sports, and pay for them all. Until then, they can shut up.

And these same people who complain about parents are the first ones who want to indoctrinate your kids, given the chance. So never feel guilty.

This *is* a war. The left knows it and has been strategizing how to conquer one social territory after the next: news media, entertainment, social media, even sports. Ultimately, their most important battleground is your child's mind. Over the decades, there have been calculated agendas and funding to advance the war.

Don't think for a moment it's been organic. It's all been very orchestrated.

Most conservative parents fail to recognize it. I can't blame them, I suppose. One day, even one year, may not seem that much different from the previous one. You've got your own work and interests. A part of you even doesn't want to believe it's happening, what with it being so absurd. Another part of you doesn't want to believe it because it would mean having to do something to fight it. People prefer complacency and inaction.

Plus, you don't want anyone to perceive you as one of those conspiracy guys. It's also hard to believe that Teacher Amanda would do or say anything devious. She's in her mid-twenties and idealistic, and she's so perky and super nice during your parent-teacher conferences. And you want everyone to think of you as one of those parents that goes along to get along and perhaps you can be influential in your own quiet and very polite way.

I understand. Very few people like confrontation.

But it doesn't matter. Suck it up. Put on your armor. Like Neo in *The Matrix*, you've seen what is really happening, and you can't unsee it. Your role in this war is to speak up, yes, but also to prop up your own young'un to be a great and knowledgeable citizen who stands up for God and America—as was the recognized role of every parent before the year 2000 or so.

If you do so, your child will forever understand the wisdom of conservatism, of the necessity of God, of getting married and having children herself one day, and of love of America and what it still stands for.

You will never have to home-school your child. You'll never have to worry that some outside force will actually influence him. The greatest gift this book might give you is the knowledge that your child will be able to go out and hold his own, no matter how strong the winds of wokism push against him.

Your child will be in that Hurricane Hunter plane, flying unphased through even the strongest and unpredictable storms.

Because you built it for him.

THE END

# ACKNOWLEDGMENTS

First and foremost, I'd like to thank my good friend David Gabor, who noticed how well I was raising my kids. He saw how stable and rock-solid they were in their love of America, God and conservative values. When I explained to him my approach to raising my kids, he encouraged—no, *insisted*—that I write this book. Without his persistent prompting, this book would never have happened. I am so grateful to him for that, as well as his invaluable recommendations and edits.

Once again, I cannot thank my good friend and publisher Chet Thompson from CT3Media enough for all his thoughts, inputs, and encouragement. Once again, he managed to put up with me for a long time on this one.

Many thanks as always to my good friends Dennis Prager and Sue Prager, both of whom have been great supporters of my work and books, as well as excellent sounding boards of my ideas and approaches. Dennis' books have also largely influenced my thinking throughout the past twenty years.

Finally, a shout-out and thanks to my kids, all of whom helped as a sounding board to many of the ideas of this book: *What are they teaching you guys? What are you hearing from your friends? What do you think?* These constant conversations were invaluable in reminding me what works and what has worked in the shaping of their values.

My engagement with my own kids appears to have worked: All of them have become stalwart and proud conservatives and believers. Incidentally, I keep the discussions going and plan to do so for the rest of their lives.

# ENDNOTES

1. Candace Hathaway, "Parents cannot 'dictate what their children are taught': School board's lawyer says parents outraged over district's transgender policy can 'choose to have your child attend elsewhere,'"https://www.theblaze.com/news/new-jersey-school-board-lawyer-tells-parents-cant-dictate-what-students-are-taught, October 26, 2022.

2. Mary Kay Linge, "Public Schools Are Teaching Our Children to Hate America," https://nypost.com/2020/02/22/public-schools-are-teaching-our-children-to-hate-america/, February 22, 2020. Much of the background in this Chapter thus far is derived from this excellent summary of the festering change in our school systems to brainwash our children.

3. Ibid.

4. Ibid.

5. Ibid.

6. Ibid.

7. Ibid.

8. See generally, Thomas Lifson, "Schoolteachers worrying about parents overhearing their brainwashing of students in online classes," https://www.americanthinker.com/blog/2020/08/schoolteachers_worrying_about_parents_overhearing_their_brainwashing_of_students_in_online_classes.html, August 11, 2020.

9. Morris M., "False Facts about the Great Wall of China You Always Thought Were True," https://www.grunge.com/52945/false-facts-great-wall-china-always-thought-true/?utm_campaign=clip. March 28, 2007.

Interestingly, as the author notes: "At other times, the Wall's defensive failures were less dramatic, but still notable. One of its primary purposes in the Ming Dynasty was to block the influx of nomadic traders and separate the Han from their supposed racial inferiors. Only it turned out the Han Chinese manning the Wall in the north weren't too bothered by nomads. They were too far from the Empire's heart. Too lonely. Too desperate to shack up with some Mongolian girls. So they just kinda let their neighbors across for trading, and then marriage, and the border just ceased to exist in any practical sense."

10. Joshua Q. Nelson, "11-year-old reads aloud from 'pornographic' book he checked out from library at school board meeting," https://nypost. com/2023/02/28/knox-zajac-reads-aloud-from-pornographic-book-at-school-board-meeting/, February 28, 2023.

11. Sabia Prescott, "Six states have now passed LGBTQ+ inclusive curriculum legislation—each with a different definition of 'inclusion,'" https://www.newamerica.org/education-policy/edcentral/six-states-have -now-passed-lgbtq-inclusive-curriculum-legislationeach-with-a-different -definition-of-inclusion/, June 17, 2021.

12. Nicola, "How Children Make Sense of the World Around Them," https://mindsofwonder.com/2016/11/24/children-make-sense-world-around/, November 24, 2016

13. Vanessa LoBue, Ph.D, "Why Children are so Good at Learning," https://www.psychologytoday.com/us/blog/the-baby-scientist/202205/why-children-are-so-good-learning, May 9, 2022.

14. Author unknown, "Steve Job Muses on What's Wrong with American Education, 1995," https://www.openculture.com/2011/11/steve_jobs_muses_on_public_education_1995.html, November 10, 2011.

15. Danielle Wallace, "Mother of NYC Heiress Paid 'Deprogrammer' Big Bucks after Daughter 'Brainwashed' by College's Woke Agenda," https://www.foxnews.com/us/mother-nyc-heiress-paid-deprogrammer-big-bucks-daughter-brainwashed-college-woke-agenda, November 27, 2022

16. Ibid.

17. Ashley Collman, "A North Korean defector says going to Columbia University reminded her of the oppressive regime, saying she felt forced to 'think the way they want you to think,'" https://news.yahoo.com/north -korean-defector-says-going-130747688.html, June 15, 2021

18. Masterclass, "What Is a Cult? 4 Types of Cults and Common Characteristics," https://www.masterclass.com/articles/what-is-a-cult#3bUrKqZ v2bhLuVVUiruyhL, November 10, 2022

19. Micaiah Bilger, "California School Has "Condom Race" Where 10-Year-Old Girls Learn How to Put On Condoms," https://www.lifenews. com/2019/06/13/california-school-has-condom-race-where-10-year-old-girls-learn-how-to-put-on-condoms/, June 13, 2019.

20. Nadine DeNinno and Ben Cost, Balenciaga Designer Deman Finally Addresses BDSM Ad Scandal, Apologizes," https://nypost.com/2022/12/02/balenciaga-designer-demna-addresses-bdsm-ad-scandal-apologizes/, December 2, 2022

21. https://en.wikipedia.org/wiki/Drag_Queen_Story_Hour

22. Wikipedia, updated as of November 26, 2022, https://en.wikipedia.org/wiki/Drag_Queen_Story_Hour

23. Jason Rafferty MD, MPH, EdM, FAAP, "Gender Identity Development in Children," https://www.healthychildren.org/English/ages-stages/

gradeschool/Pages/Gender-Identity-and-Gender-Confusion-In-Children.aspx

24. Joe Biden "Rose Garden" speech, "Remarks by President Biden and First Lady Jill Biden at the 2023 National and State Teachers of the Year Celebration,"https://www.whitehouse.gov/briefing-room/speeches-remarks/2023/04/24/remarks-by-president-biden-and-first-lady-jill-biden-at-the-2023-national-and-state-teachers-of-the-year-celebration/, April 24, 2023/

25. Author unknown, https://worldpopulationreview.com/country-rankings/most-hated-country, 2022

26. Author unknown, "2022 Index of Economic Freedom," https://www.heritage.org/index/ranking, 2022.

27. See generally, Allie Griffin, "California panel estimates $569 billion in reparations is owed to black residents," https://nypost.com/2022/12/02/california-panel-estimates-569-billion-in-reparations-is-owed-to-black-residents/, December 2, 2022. The article describes how Governor Gavin Newsom of California created a "task force" to study the propriety of such reparations.

28. John Walker, "A Volcano Eruption Can Emit More $CO_2$ Than All Humanity. Why Worry?", https://principia-scientific.com/a-volcano-eruption-can-emit-more-co2-than-all-humanity-why-worry/, February 12, 2020.

29. See, e.g., University Of Colorado At Boulder, "Global Sea Levels Likely To Rise Higher In 21st Century Than Previous Predictions," https://www.sciencedaily.com/releases/2002/02/020220075633.htm, February 20, 2002; Author unknown, "Anticipating Future Sea Levels," https://earthobservatory.nasa.gov/images/148494/anticipating-future-sea-levels; 2021; Jane Lee, "Sea Level to Rise up to a Foot by 2050, Interagency Report Finds," https://climate.nasa.gov/news/3146/sea-level-to-rise-up-to-a-foot-by-2050-interagency-report-finds/, February 15, 2022; "Sea-level rise could nearly double over earlier estimates in next 100 years," https://www.sciencedaily.com/releases/2016/03/160330130804.htm, March 30, 2016

30. John Keefe and Rachel Ramirez, "Our underwater future: What sea level rise will look like around the globe," https://www.cnn.com/2021/10/12/world/3-degrees-sea-level-rise-climate-central/index.html, October 12, 2021

31. Chris Mooney, "Humans Have Already Set in Motion 69 Feet of Sea Level Rise," https://www.motherjones.com/environment/2013/01/climate-desk-greenland-and-69-feet-sea-level-rise/, January 31, 2013.

32. Walker, *Op cit.* (regarding volcanoes); Sophie Lewis, "NASA: Moon "wobble" in orbit may lead to record flooding on Earth,"https://www.cbsnews.com/news/nasa-moon-wobble-orbit-record-flooding-earth-sea-level-rise-climate-change/, July 15, 2021 (regarding moon's impact on sea levels).

33. Dana Nuccitelli, "The 97% v the 3% – just how much global warming are humans causing?" https://www.theguardian.com/environment/climate-consensus-97-per-cent/2014/sep/15/97-vs-3-how-much-global-warming-are-humans-causing, September 15, 2014.

34. Alan Buis, "The Raw Truth on Global Temperature Records," https://climate.nasa.gov/ask-nasa-climate/3071/the-raw-truth-on-global-temperature-records/, March 25, 2021. Even NASA seems to acknowledge this obvious point: New technology means that temperature data needs to be constantly adjusted. As NASA puts it specifically, "ensuring the accuracy of Earth's long-term global and regional surface temperature records is a challenging, constantly evolving undertaking. There are lots of reasons for this, including changes in the availability of data, technological advancements in how land and sea surface temperatures are measured, the growth of urban areas, and changes to where and when temperature data are collected, to name just a few. Over time, these changes can lead to measurement inconsistencies that affect temperature data records."

35. Author unknown, "Report: China emissions exceed all developed nations combined," https://www.bbc.com/news/world-asia-57018837, May 7, 2021

36. Daily.com Reporter, "Climate change warrior Al Gore's Nashville estate expends '21 times more energy than the average US home uses per year,'" https://www.dailymail.co.uk/news/article-4758152/Al-Gore-s-mansion-uses-21-times-energy-average.html, August 3, 2017. Not surprisingly, the left-wing Snopes.com addresses this argument and says it is "mixed" in its veracity. It argues that it's not 21 times more carbon emitting, but more like ... 12 times. Also, they make other excuses for the Gores: the Gores also use the house for their business purposes, so it's only natural that it would emit more carbon. I'm surprised they didn't also argue that Gore is doing so much for the planet, presumably he should be able to partially burn it to save it.

37. Rick Mayer, "A Johns Hopkins study says 'ill-founded' COVID lockdowns did more harm than good,"https://health.wusf.usf.edu/health-news-florida/2022-02-02/a-johns-hopkins-study-says-ill-founded-lockdowns-did-little-to-limit-covid-deaths, February 2, 2022

38. Brendan Cole, "Antibody Study Shows COVID-19 Rate of Infection May Be up to 85 Times Higher Than Reported," https://www.newsweek.com/covid-19-coronavirus-antibodies-infection-higher-1498740, April 18, 2020; See also, https://www.nytimes.com/2020/05/14/opinion/coronavirus-research-misinformation.html. The New York Times couldn't wait to say how "The Right" was "seizing" this fact. As if it would be wrong for them to claim that we should stay the course of panic, despite the new information.

39. Editorial Board, Investor Business Daily, "Is There Anything Environmentalists Won't Blame On Climate Change?" https://www.investors.com/politics/editorials/environmentalists-climate-change-blame/, December 12, 2018.

40. Ibid.

41. U.S. Department of Agriculture, "A Look at Agricultural Productivity Growth in the United States, 1948-2017," https://www.usda.gov/media/blog/2020/03/05/look-agricultural-productivity-growth-united-states-1948-2017, July 29, 2021.

42. Lisa Zollinger, "27 Historical Events that Shaped Modern Plumbing Systems," https://www.iveyengineering.com/historical-events-plumbing -systems/ circa 2014

43. For this and an otherwise fascinating history of internal plumbing, see Lisa Zollinger, *op cit.*

44. Author unknown, "Israeli Inventions Benefit the World," https:// www.factsaboutisrael.uk/israeli-inventions/, circa 2018.

45. Wikipedia, "List of Israeli Inventions and Discoveries," https:// en.wikipedia.org/wiki/List_of_Israeli_inventions_and_discoveries, updated January 29, 2023

46. Joe Hasell and Max Roser, "How do we know the history of extreme poverty?," https://ourworldindata.org/extreme-history-methods, February 05, 2019

47. Author unknown, "Decline of Global Extreme Poverty Continues but Has Slowed: World Bank,"https://www.worldbank.org/en/news/ press-release/2018/09/19/decline-of-global-extreme-poverty-continues-but- has-slowed-world-bank, September 19, 2018.

48. Aaron Bandler, "5 Statistics Showing How Capitalism Solves Poverty," https://www.dailywire.com/news/5-statistics-showing-how-capitalism -solves-poverty-aaron-bandler, March 18, 2017.

49. Ibid.

50. Ibid.

51. Ibid.

52. Steven Horwitz, "Capitalism is good for the poor," https://fee.org/ articles/capitalism-is-good-for-the-poor/, June 9, 2016

53. Daniel J. Mitchell, "Poverty in the U.S. Was Plummeting—Until Lyndon Johnson Declared War On It," https://fee.org/articles/poverty-in-the- us-was-plummeting-until-lyndon-johnson-declared-war-on-it/, October 16, 2018.

54. BBC report segment, from Youtube: https://www.youtube.com/ watch?v=8MGbyLUCw5k

55. BBC segment, YouTube video: https://www.youtube.com/watch?v =HAttn-5lM3Y

56. Marian Tupy, "Countries That Transitioned Rapidly From Communism to Capitalism Fare Better," https://reason.com/2016/07/19/countries -that-transitioned-rapidly-from/ July 19, 2016.

57. Nima Sanandaji, "Nordic Countries Aren't Actually Socialist,"https://foreignpolicy.com/2021/10/27/nordic-countries-not-socialist -denmark-norway-sweden-centrist/, October 27, 2021

58. Ibid.

59. "GDP Per Capita -Israel," https://data.worldbank.org/indicator/ NY.GDP.PCAP.CD?locations=IL," updated 2021. See also, Abigail Klein Leichman, "Why Israel Rocks at Commericializing Academic Innovations," https://www.israel21c.org/why-israel-rocks-at-commercializing-academic -innovations/, January 18, 2018

60. Department of Energy, "75 Breakthroughs by America's National Laboratories," https://www.energy.gov/articles/75-breakthroughs-americas-national-laboratories-0, February 14, 2018.

61. Author unknown, "America's Cultural Role in the World Today," https://access-internationalvg2.cappelendamm.no/c951212/artikkel/vis.html?tid=385685, circa 2007

62. Michael de Sapio, "The Importance of American Art," https://theimaginativeconservative.org/2019/07/importance-american-art-michael-de-sapio.html, July 5, 2019

63. Wikipedia, https://en.wikipedia.org/wiki/Visual_art_of_the_United_States, as of February 7, 2023.

64. "America's Cultural Role in the World Today," *Op cit.*

65. Ibid.

66. Ashley Ross, "The Surprising Way a Supermarket Changed the World," https://time.com/4480303/supermarkets-history/, September 9, 2016.

67. Robert Whaples, "Hours of Work in U.S. History," https://eh.net/encyclopedia/hours-of-work-in-u-s-history/

68. Author unknown, "Immigration to United States vs. Other Countries," https://immigrationlawyerslosangeles.com/blog/immigration-united-states-vs-countries/, circa 2023. The figures represented are as of 2015. The numbers have surely increased since then.

69. Jon Clifton, "150 Million Adults Worldwide Would Migrate to the U.S.," https://news.gallup.com/poll/153992/150-Million-Adults-Worldwide-Migrate.aspx, April 20, 2012.

70. Ewan Palmer, "FBI Under Pressure for Targeting Catholics in Leaked Document," https://www.newsweek.com/fbi-memo-catholics-radical-traditional-leaked-1780379, February 10, 2023.

71. Arielle Del Turco, "Hostility Against Churches Is on the Rise in the United States," https://downloads.frc.org/EF/EF22L24.pdf, December, 2022

72. Hannah Frishberg, "American church attendance hits historic low, says Gallup survey," https://nypost.com/2021/03/30/american-church-attendance-hits-historic-low-survey/, March 20, 2021.

73. Ibid.

74. Adam Gabbatt, "Losing their religion: why US churches are on the decline," https://www.theguardian.com/us-news/2023/jan/22/us-churches-closing-religion-covid-christianity, January 22, 2023

75. Chris Phelan, "College Athlete Wins $100,000 Settlement After She Refuses to Kneel for National Anthem," https://www.msn.com/en-us/tv/news/college-athlete-wins-100-000-settlement-after-she-refuses-to-kneel-for-national-anthem/ar-AA16bQhC, February 21, 2023

76. Lee Duigon, "Red Cross Fires Christian Who Opposed 'Gay Pride' Month," https://chalcedon.edu/resources/articles/red-cross-fires-christian-who-opposed-gay-pride-month, August 15, 2005

77. Ingrid Jacques, "Stanford's political correctness czars deem 'American' and 'guys' harmful words (no joke)," https://www.usatoday.com/story/opinion/columnist/2023/01/03/stanford-language-police

-decide-american-offensive-word/10961282002/, January 3, 2023. Stanford eventually backed down and withdrew the proposed list of offensive words after considerable pushback, but the point is that tried and thought it would gain traction. This is an example of how pushback against the left is easy enough—but you have to actually *do* it.

78. Philip Goff, "Our Improbable Existence Is No Evidence for a Multiverse," https://www.scientificamerican.com/article/our-improbable-existence-is-no-evidence-for-a-multiverse/, January 10, 2021

79. Ibid.

80. Watchtower Online Library, "Chapter 4: Could Life Originate by Chance?" https://wol.jw.org/en/wol/d/r1/lp-e/1101985014, date unknown

81. Ibid.

82. Phillip E. Johnson, "Fact, Myth, and the Scopes Monkey Trial," https://www.discovery.org/a/fact-myth-and-the-scopes-monkey-trial/, July 1, 1997.

83. Marshall Brain, "How Evolution Works," https://science.howstuff works.com/life/evolution/evolution1.htm, date unknown

84. Ibid.

85. Author unknown, "Why Some Scientists Believe in God," https://www.jw.org/en/library/magazines/g20040622/Why-Some-Scientists-Believe-in-God/, June 22, 2004

86. For an excellent description of the argument as to the creation of the universe and the sequence of the arrival of life forms on earth and life itself, as well as of the Cambrian explosion below, I urge you to read *The Science of God*, by Gerald Schroeder (2009).

87. Ibid.

88. Reviewed by Jack Turban, M.D., M.H.S, "What is Gender Dysphoria?" https://www.psychiatry.org/patients-families/gender-dysphoria/what-is-gender-dysphoria, August 2022

89. Psychology Today staff, "Gender Dysphoria," https://www.psychologytoday.com/us/conditions/gender-dysphoria, October 25, 2021, Psychology Today makes the assumption—without support—that "[b]ecause these estimates are based on the number of people who seek formal treatment—including hormone therapy and gender confirmation surgery—these rates are likely an underestimate."

90. Laurel Duggan, "Growing Body Of Evidence Shows What's Really Causing Rapid Onset of Gender Dysphoria in Teens," https://www.westernjournal.com/growing-body-evidence-shows-really-causing-rapid-onset-gender-dysphoria-teens/, November 25, 2022.

91. Ibid.

92. Ibid.

93. Kiara Alfonseca, "Anti-transgender sentiment follows Nashville shooting," https://abcnews.go.com/US/anti-transgender-sentiment-nashville-shooting/story?id=98177377, March 28, 2023

94. Jarryd Jaeger, "Leftist Wayne State professor suspended after writing that speakers invited by conservative students should be killed

rather than shouted down," https://thepostmillennial.com/wayne-state-prof
-suspended-after-claiming-it-is-far-more-admirable-to-kill-ideological
-opponents-than-talk-to-them, March 30, 2032.

95. Jeff Zymeri, "Arizona Governor's Press Secretary Out after Tweet
Encouraging Violence against 'Transphobes,'" https://www.msn.com/
en-us/news/politics/arizona-governors-press-secretary-out-after-tweet
-encouraging-violence-against-transphobes/ar-AA19ezis, March 29, 2023.

96. Cortney Weil, "Days after Nashville shooting, Wyoming Dem sides
with Antifa, implies supporting gun violence against those who oppose
'trans' agenda," https://www.theblaze.com/news/days-after-nashville-shoot
ing-wyoming-dem-sides-with-antifa-implies-supporting-gun-violence-
against-those-who-oppose-trans-agenda, April 3, 2023.

97. See e.g., Brodigan, "HS Teacher Put on Leave for Assigning Essay
About 9-Year-Old Girls Watching Man Masturbate to Completion," https://
www.louderwithcrowder.com/teacher-leave-assignment-tenth-grade,
October 19, 2022; Brodigan, "Teacher Sends Kindergarten Students Home
with Homework to List Best Places in Their Houses to Masturbate,"
https://www.louderwithcrowder.com/kindergarten-outrage-homework
-assignment, May 15, 2022

98. Joe Kort, PhD, "Drag Queen Story Time for Children," https://www.
psychologytoday.com/us/blog/understanding-the-erotic-code/201901/
drag-queen-storytime-children, January 23, 2019.

99. "Young Children Are Being Targeted With Sexual Content. The
Equality Act Would Make It Worse," Jared Eckert and Makenna McCoy,
https://www.heritage.org/marriage-and-family/commentary/young
-children-are-being-targeted-sexual-content-the-equality-act, June 21, 2021,
citing Bonnie Young, The Impact of Timing of Pornography Exposure on
Mental Health, Life Satisfaction, and Sexual Behavior," Brigham Young
University, BYU Scholars Archive, May 1, 2017 (accessible through https://
scholarsarchive.byu.edu/cgi/viewcontent.cgi?article=7727&context=etd).

100. Tara Campbell, "Bay Area LGBTQ+ community responds to SJ
Sharks' goalie refusing to wear Pride-themed jersey," https://abc7news.
com/james-reimer-san-jose-sharks-pride-jersey-night-bay-area-lgbtq
-community/12976151/, March 19, 2023.

101. Mike LaChance, "State of Oregon Denies Woman's Application
to Adopt Based on Her Christian Faith," https://www.thegatewaypundit.
com/2023/04/state-of-oregon-denies-womans-application-to-adopt-based-
on-her-christian-faith/, April 5, 2023.

102. Reuters, "School's Transgender Policy Trumped Teacher's Religious Rights, U.S. Court Rules," https://www.usnews.com/news/top-
news/articles/2023-04-07/schools-transgender-policy-trumped-teachers
-religious-rights-u-s-court-rules, April 7, 2023.

103. Joe Hoft, ""Parental Rights End When You Send Your Kids
to Public School" – New Mexico Attorney In Training Session to Teachers,"https://www.thegatewaypundit.com/2023/03/parental-rights-end

-when-you-send-your-kids-to-public-school-new-mexico-attorney-in-training-session-to-teachers-video/, 2023

104. Cullen Linebarger, "'State Sanctioned Kidnapping' — California Democrat Pushes Bill That Would Allow Therapists to Snatch Children From Parents Without Trial," https://www.thegatewaypundit.com/2023/03/state-sanctioned-kidnapping-california-democrat-pushes-bill-that-would-allow-therapists-to-snatch-children-from-parents-without-trial/, Mar. 26, 2023. Specifically, the bill's language provides: "The mental health treatment or counseling of a minor authorized by this section shall include involvement of the minor's parent or guardian unless the professional person who is treating or counseling the minor, after consulting with the minor, determines that the involvement would be inappropriate."

105. Washington State Legislature, SB 5599, Session 2023-24, https://app.leg.wa.gov/billsummary?BillNumber=5599&Year=2023&Initiative=False#documentSection

# ABOUT THE AUTHOR

BARAK LURIE is the managing partner of the law firm Lurie & Kramer in Los Angeles, California. Barak obtained his BA with honors from Stanford University in 1985, and his JD and MBA from the UCLA School of Law and Anderson School of Business in 1989. He also hosted The Barak Lurie Show, the most listened to radio program on weekend AM radio in Los Angeles. He also guest-hosts for several other programs, including The Dennis Prager Show.

Barak has written several bestsellers: *Atheism Kills, Atheism Destroys,* and *Rise of the Sex Machines*. All of his books, as well as his many articles, podcasts, and speeches, call for our collective need for faith and return to conservative values.

Barak is a devout lover of America and Israel, an avid mountain biker and vegan. He and his wife Stacey have three America-loving and God-loving children. He says the greatest compliment he has ever received is when people remark on how well-behaved, kind, and conservative his kids are.

Made in the USA
Middletown, DE
02 September 2023

37827754R00106